OXFORD (c. 1756)

WADHAM
COLLEGE

St. Cross
Church

ST. CROSS ROAD

Music Room

HOLYWELL STREET

HERTFORD
COLL

ndon
ilding

OLD CITY

MAGDALEN

heldonian
Th.

Bodleian
Lib

NEW COLLEGE

St. Peter's
in the East

GROVE

LONGWALL STREET

(DEER PARK)

Radcliffe
Camera

ALL SOULS

QUEEN'S

ST.
EDMUND
HALL

B
N
C

St.
Mary's
Ch.

COLLEGE

COLLEGE

MAGDALEN

HIGH STREET

ADDISON'S WALK

MAGPIE LANE

UNIVERSITY
COLLEGE

COLLEGE

KING EDWARD ST.

ORIEL

ORIEL

COLLEGE

MERTON STREET

CORPUS
CHRISTI
COLL

MERTON
COLLEGE

Physic Garden

MAGDALEN BR.

HEADING
TO CO

Cathedral

D1221952

BROAD W

CHRIST

CHURCH

MEADOW

A

POCKET COMPANION

FOR

OXFORD

A Facsimile Reprint

Edited with an Introduction
and Appendix
by

JAMES L. *and*
CONNIE C. THORSON

Printed for Blackwell North America, Inc.,
and B. H. Blackwell, Ltd.
by Graphic Arts Center in Portland, Oregon, 1988.

ACKNOWLEDGEMENT
The endpaper maps are reproduced with the kind per-
mission of Oxford University Press.

PREFACE

Having the opportunity to add some modern comments on and adjustments to *A Pocket Companion for Oxford* has been, most of all, an enormous pleasure. Visiting Oxford frequently, as we have been fortunate to do, we know that the city of Oxford cannot really be separated from the University of Oxford. The modern city contains an industrial base and a market economy that crowd the streets with people, but those streets are also crowded with students, teachers, and researchers from all over Great Britain and much of the rest of the world as well. Through the years that we have been visiting Oxford, we not only have been struck by the occasional changes but also by the continuity that remains within those changes. The city has grown but still provides green belts along the rivers that characterized it in 1756, despite suburban developments nearby. The University has also changed, as science and engineering subjects have evolved into major areas of study and research with all their necessary laboratories and support facilities.

The realization that few things have really changed (though things have been added) is what, we hope, will encourage the visitor to use, with fair success, a mid-eighteenth-century guidebook to see what is now, of course, a late twentieth-century city and university. Another realization that the visitor who stays long enough to experience Oxford (not just the few minutes one has on a day trip from London to Stratford) will reach is that the real reason for the existence of the University is for education and research. It was not built as a tourist attraction; being a tourist attraction is only incidental to its primary reason for surviving and thriving. One wonders what the founders of the thirteenth-century establishments would think of Oxford's magnetic appeal today. In 1756, just as now, visiting Oxford meant visiting the University. Most guides to Oxford, old and new, concentrate on the Colleges and other institutions affiliated with the University because they, above all else, give Oxford its unique flavor, educationally and aesthetically.

In the minds of many people, even those who have never had the pleasure of visiting Oxford, Blackwell's and Oxford are inextricably linked. The long and supportive association of the bookseller with the city and University makes this new edition of *A Pocket Companion for Oxford* by the Blackwell firm a natural endeavor. We want to take this opportunity to thank Miles Blackwell, Blackwell's Chairman, and Jack Walsdorf and Chris Tyzack for their active support and encouragement. The project would have been difficult to complete without access to the collections of the Bodleian Library and the Oxford County Library (Westgate Center) and without the support of the Research Allocations Committee at the University of New Mexico. The person who ultimately deserves our warmest thanks, however, is Karina Williamson, Fellow of St. Hilda's College, Oxford, who so generously presented the crown of our collection of guides to Oxford, *A Pocket Companion for Oxford* (1756), to us in 1980. Our having this delightful book made the project possible.

INTRODUCTION

This volume, unlike many facsimile reprints of works originally published in earlier eras, is intended for the general public rather than the specialized student or expert. It should be particularly interesting and useful to the visitor to Oxford, whether the visit be an actual one or only in the memory or imagination. The ancient university town near the confluence of the Cherwell and Thames rivers has long been a mecca for students, scholars, and tourists. The present volume was intended for the third audience when it first came out in the middle of the eighteenth century, and its republication now, though not devoid of antiquarian and scholarly interest, is meant to provide pleasure for the modern tourist and reader.

With that in mind, the present editors have tried to restrain their scholarly garrulousness and to let the book speak for itself. The amazing fact is that it remains extremely relevant to the geography, history, and particularly to the architecture of Oxford after nearly two and a half centuries. These few pages of introduction, the footnotes to the text, and the appendix which we have added at the end of the book are not meant to supersede the volume itself but rather to enhance it by bringing it up to date while setting it firmly in its own historical context as well.

Social historians and historical bibliographers have long noticed a radical change that came over English society in the seventeenth and eighteenth centuries. While travel both to international destinations (the grand tour being the most obvious example) and to domestic places of resort had been largely restricted to the upper classes and their attendant servants in eras prior to the Restoration of Charles II to the throne of England in 1660, the century that followed that event was to see an enormous growth in leisure time and discretionary money among that amorphous and ill-defined group known as the middle class. It was this body of potential customers, anxious for both instruction and recreation, toward which this volume and its predecessors and successors (and they are legion) were aimed.

Several other strands fit into the fabric that makes up the background for the book. They include an interest in English antiquities, an interest which was not divorced from a certain amount of English chauvinism, and, on the other hand, the laudable desire of booksellers to make an honest living and support their families by selling books, in this instance, in Oxford. The stimuli for the production of travel literature are largely made up of a mixture of these motives.

One of the giant names in the history of the study of English antiquities is that of William Camden (1551-1623). He was an antiquarian and historian from Oxford whose long list of publications, almost all originally in Latin, is quite impressive. His most important work for our purposes is usually called Camden's *Britannia*. It was first published in two volumes in 1586, but it was often augmented by Camden himself and by others. It described all of Great Britain and Ireland and their antiquities. The 1722 translation of Camden into English was the source for some of the information and misinformation in *A Pocket Companion*.

That Camden wrote in Latin is presumptive proof that he defined his audience as the learned community of his time, but that his work was translated into the vernacular further proves that others believed that it would appeal to a wider audience as well. In the 1722 English version, which consists of two large folio volumes, the section pertaining to Oxford is to be found in Volume I, pp. 303-314. The anonymous writer (or perhaps editor or compiler might be more accurate terms) of our volume admits his debt to his scholarly predecessor when he quotes from "Campden" concerning the foundation of the Bodleian Library (pp. 10 ff.

below), but at least some of the other material in this book about the history of Oxford and its Colleges comes from Camden, though often with an intermediate step.

The intermediate step in most cases was another prolific author, Thomas Salmon (1679-1767), who was also an antiquary, a geographer, and an historian, though not nearly so famous as Camden. Salmon wrote in English and his histories, geographical gazetteers, and the most pertinent volume, *The Present State of the Universities,* were obviously intended for a somewhat wider audience than merely those who read Latin.

Salmon also had at least one eye cocked toward his own financial well-being, as the title page of *The Present State of the Universities* contains a rather unusual statement for the period. At the bottom of the page, the place of publication, London, is followed by these words: "Printed for the sole Benefit of the Author, and sold by J. Roberts in *Warwick-Lane*. 1744." The bold assertion of the proprietary (and pecuniary) rights of the author to the benefits of his creative labors is quite unusual at this early point in the history of publishing. Such authorial rights were not recognized by statute at the time, and, in this case, as nearly as we can determine, his rights were violated almost immediately, as we shall point out below. The title page also boasts that the volume is *"By Mr. Salmon, Author of Modern History,"* a typical ploy to impress potential buyers with Salmon's popular reputation.

Salmon's 476 page volume has yet another slightly misleading feature on its title page. It presents itself as Volume I of an ambitious longer work: *The Present State of the Universities and of the Five Adjacent Counties of Cambridge, Huntington, Bedford, Buckingham and Oxford.* The "first" volume (and actually the only) promises to cover the county and city of Oxford, its Colleges and the history of the University "continued down to the present times" as well as to feature such practical advice as "the Method of obtaining Degrees" and "Remarks on University Education, and a College Life, with the Expence attending it."

Though apparently not educated at a university, Salmon resided in Cambridge for some time and traveled very extensively for his time, having even circumnavigated the globe around 1740 with Admiral, later Lord, Anson. The "Modern History" to which the title page alludes is probably his best-known work, published in 1739 as *Modern History, or the Present State of all Nations . . . illustrated with Cuts and Maps . . . by Herman Moll*. Though not much can be learned about his life, it is apparent that he was a Grub-street hack, that is, one who earned his living, often precariously, by his pen. He published some twenty works, many of them multi-volumed, between 1722 and 1759.

Unfortunately for Salmon, his *The Present State of the Universities* apparently did not become a best-seller and make his fortune. Further volumes in the projected series seem never to have appeared, and even the "first" was not republished, although some of the material in it was to reappear in a number of forms, including the present volume.

In 1747, or at least so its title page asserts, one M. Cooper of Pater-noster Row in London caused a new volume to be printed entitled *The Gentleman and Lady's Pocket Companion for Oxford*. Mary Cooper was the widow of Thomas Cooper, one of the most prolific of the publishers of pamphlet literature of the period. Her name appears alone on many publications after her husband's death about 1743. This small volume of seventy-one pages is a direct antecedent of the present volume. Though published by Mrs. Cooper in London, it was also to be "sold by Mr. Clements and Mr. Fletcher in Oxford." James Fletcher was a "privilegiatus bookseller" to the University from 1730 onward until his death at age eighty-five in 1795. His shop was in the Turl, and he was an important figure in the literary life of Oxford at the time. In 1757 a catalogue of his publications ran to over one hundred titles, but he was not a principal in the present volume, which was taken over solely by Mr. Richard Clements, of whom not so much is known. In some imprints, as in this current one, he is said to have his shop "near the theatre," which is the Sheldonian Theatre in Oxford, and it may be that he was located on the site of one of B. H. Blackwell's current locations in the Broad Street that runs by the Theatre, but we have been unable to locate his shop with any confidence. He was the son of another Oxford Bookseller, Mr. Henry Clements. Then, as now, bookselling often ran in families.

This 1747 volume redacts a good deal of Salmon's book of 1744 without attribution, but presents the material in a much more compact form. While it may seem mean to criticize Salmon so many years after his effort, the 1744 book is ponderous, scattered in its effects, and frankly, dull in its overall impact on the reader. Though professedly about the "state of the Universities," Salmon allows himself to go on for many pages on the Duke of Marlborough's part in the War of the Spanish Succession (1698-1713), on ministerial and royal mismanagement during that war, and on other historical material of little direct effect on the state of the universities and of absolutely no use or interest to the tourist. He omits mention of Cambridge, despite his title.

There is a brief Preface to the 1747 book that claims that this new *Companion* is parallel to the "Accounts of Curiosities" or "Descriptions" of Paris or Rome that greeted visitors to those cities. The book promises to serve as an expediter for seeing Oxford, "the most celebrated University in the Kingdom" and as an aid in retaining memories of it. It will also provide "Information to those who see all the World at home." We hope that our twentieth-century readers may enjoy the same benefits from this republication.

In 1748, Salmon published *The Foreigner's Companion Through the Universities of Cambridge and Oxford ...* London: Printed for William Owen, 1748. The new book does have sections (quite discrete from each other) devoted to each of the ancient English Universities, unlike the 1744 volume. In the new book, the Oxford descriptions are often lifted entire from the earlier work, but far less extraneous material is included. The entire Oxford section, printed and paginated separately from the Cambridge section which precedes it, numbers only ninety-seven pages despite being supplemented by lists of "Bishops and Eminent Men" for most of the Colleges.

The title page again is curious, as there is no attempt whatsoever in the book to explain the English institutions to its purported foreign audience. This particular title may have been invented merely to distinguish it from similar books that were coming on the market and were to do so in increasing numbers in the 1750s. It is clear that, exactly as today, various publishers brought out companions, guides, and other works to tempt the tourist. There was such a proliferation, in fact, that Thomas Warton, the poet, historian and professor of poetry, and Fellow of Trinity College, Oxford, published a spoof on them called *A Companion to the Guide and a Guide to the Companion* in about 1760.

To return to Mr. Salmon, the change in title pages between 1744 and 1748 is probably indicative of a change in the relationship between author and publisher. In 1744 the author seems to have taken the risk in hopes of the profit, while the 1748 volume seems to have reverted to the more common practice in which a bookseller, William Owen, a prominent one in this case, causes a book to be printed.

In addition to the 1747 borrowing of Salmon's material, the editors of *The London Magazine* also raided

Salmon's store of facts and printed some extracts ver-
batim in a half-dozen pages late in that year. In 1748,
Salmon responded to these unauthorized publications on
the verso of the title page of *The Foreigner's Companion*.
The notice reads:

> N.B. *The Pamphlet, intituled,* The Gentleman
> and Lady's Pocket Companion for *Oxford,*
> was *taken verbatim from* The Present State of
> the University of Oxford, *published by Mr.*
> Salmon *in* 1743 [sic.]. *The* London Magazine
> *has also taken the Liberty to transcribe Part of the*
> Present State of *Oxford. But neither of these*
> *Plagiaries have been so just to acknowledge from*
> *whence they copied it.*

This rather testy note may have achieved its desired
result. It is only speculation, but when Richard Clements
started publishing the earliest version of his *A Pocket
Companion* in 1753, he may well have come to an
agreement, probably financial, with Salmon and Owen
about the rights to the material in the earlier books, as the
issue never seems to have been raised again.

The 1756 edition, reproduced here, says that it is a
"new Edition, with Additions," and an examination of
the changes between it and its various predecessors supports that assertion. Some unknown hand, perhaps
Clements', went through the volume and imposed essentially four kinds of changes on the materials at hand:
there are insertions of new holders of positions, minor
verbal variations to make the volume read more fluidly,
substitutions of more accurate observations for more
general ones (382 feet for the 120 yards for the length of
the front of Christ Church, for instance), and, most
interesting perhaps, suppression of almost all of Salmon's
negative observations about Oxford. The general tone of
the new edition, much more up-beat and positive than
Salmon's original, engages the sympathy and reinforces
the pleasure of the interested tourist.

The format of the present book and its ancestors in 1753 and 1754 is much more convenient than the smaller size of the 1747 edition, the first one with which Clements is associated, though only as one of the sellers of Mary Cooper's book in Oxford. We hope that it will feel good to the hand and tantalizing to the eye and mind of its twentieth-century readers.

The first thing that many modern readers will notice is the "long s" which was a convention of English printed books of this and ealier periods. English printers used a type character for the lower case *s* which resembles and is hard to distinguish from the lower case *f*. This convention, which was finally discarded later in the eighteenth century, is easy to adjust to and should act as a clear reminder that the words, though relevant to the modern tourist and reader, were first published in the middle of the eighteenth century.

The University of Oxford resembles in many ways any important modern university, but it has, along with its sister university, Cambridge, some features that are extremely distinctive, if not unique. The separate Colleges, each with its independent foundation, buildings, endowment, and administration, are the most important of these features, and the ones which appear most immediately to the learned observer and the tourist alike. American tourists, upon arriving in Oxford, often ask "where is the campus" or "where is the University," and the usual response is something like "it's all around you," or "there is no campus," or something even more frivolous. The point is that the University is really an abstract concept which existed for over a hundred years before it purchased its first real estate. At the time of *A Pocket Companion* it still had only six buildings, all of which are described in pages 7 through 22 below. Libraries take a large share in those public buildings of the University, and the modern visitor should be prepared for even more, as the extensive and rich collections housed in the

Bodleian Library and its branches are supplemented by libraries for each of the thirty-five Colleges, by numerous libraries dedicated to the work of individual faculties (The English Faculty Library in the St. Cross Building comes to mind as an example), and by many other specialized libraries in Oxford. There is a good book on the subject, Paul Morgan's *Oxford Libraries outside of the Bodleian* (Second Edition, 1980).

One of the joys of touring Oxford is that despite the statements of the local specialists that there is *no* campus, these old university buildings all lie in a very small area between the Broad and the High, an area largely uncluttered by automotive traffic. Even if one has only a few hours, it is possible to visit them as well as several of the Colleges which are also in the same area. Thus it is possible to see several monuments to English history and architecture without resorting to automotive transportation.

Concerning the architecture, we will only note that Christopher Wren, one of the most famous of English architects, was Professor of Astronomy at Oxford when he turned his hand to designing his first building, the Sheldonian Theatre, seen by some as his greatest triumph. His work and the work of many other architects makes walking around Oxford a continual joy. We have not tried to provide as much detail for the centuries since *A Pocket Companion* as it provided for its own and previous times, as there are detailed architectural guides available for those who desire them.

The Colleges, already a very impressive physical presence in Oxford at the time of *A Pocket Companion*, continue to be a beautiful feature of the urban landscape. We have provided what we hope will be helpful notes to the 1756 descriptions, but have not annotated the many names listed in the *Companion* as professors, vice-chancellors, heads of houses, and other University officers.

The lists give the modern reader an idea of the scope of the institution as it was in 1756. If one's curiosity is piqued about the present, the *Oxford University Pocket Diary*, published annually by Oxford University Press, will provide an accurate list of the officers, including professors, readers, and directors of institutes that make up the University as well as fairly thorough information on the officers of the Colleges. We have not defined words whose meaning is reasonably clear from the context, though occasionally meanings have changed somewhat.

The benefactions given to Colleges and institutions of the University are often listed in detail, and the small size of some of those mentioned may be almost laughable in our inflated times, but it might be useful to recall that one authority suggested at about the same period that a student could get along at Oxford, tuition, room, and board for £32 per annum. Amounts are occasionally given in Marks, a now obsolete measure of coinage equal to two-thirds of a pound, or in shillings and pence, divisions of one-twentieth of a pound and one-twelfth of a shilling, divisions in use until recently. Most of the geographical limitations on fellowships and scholarships at the various Colleges no longer pertain, and most of them have a distinctly international flavor at this time.

We have not verified the lists of paintings and sculpture, as these have a habit of moving about within Colleges. Several of the paintings listed as being in the Principal's Lodgings and the Library of Jesus College are now to be seen in the Hall, for instance. In most cases, works of art are still in the possession of the institutions, though their locations may have changed, and in many Colleges portraits of recent prominent members have been added.

Almost every College has a hall, where its members dine, a library, and a chapel, and from these features and the quadrangles of housing for students and fellows each

College takes on its own special flavor. In 1756, all of the Colleges were within a few hundred yards of Bodley, but expansion has forced newer Colleges further from the center. The new Colleges are listed in the Appendix, where they are grouped in accordance with walking itineraries. The *Companion* itself is also organized on that implicit principle. The itineraries devised by the author are easy to follow, especially with the aid of a map.

We have added two maps to the end papers of the present edition, one of modern Oxford and the other of Oxford in 1756 to show those buildings which are mentioned in *A Pocket Companion*. Either may be used to get around to the Colleges, especially the older ones, but the modern one should be consulted to find one's way to and through the newer Colleges.

The original "perspective views" have been reproduced, as they still pertain exactly to the tour of Oxford. After some deliberation, we have decided not to introduce any modern pictures, as they might detract from the effect of the old guidebook in the modern tourist's hand. We are also fully conscious of how photogenic Oxford is for the modern tourist with camera in hand.

We hope that exploring and discovering both the city and the University of Oxford, with *A Pocket Companion for Oxford* in hand, will bring delight to the visitor. Whether seeing Oxford for the first time or the tenth, the visitor will, we trust, be caught up in its vibrant, exciting atmosphere. It is our desire that *A Pocket Companion* will add to the tourist's enjoyment of a fascinating city and University whose educational, cultural, and political past is reflected in nearly every architectural marvel today. While there are new buildings sandwiched in between the old in very ingenious and clever ways, mainly because the institutional life of the University and the Colleges demands continued expansion and modernization, we have not attempted to list them all. They are part of the expected evolution of the University and do not change the raison d'etre or the traditions of the old or new establishments; they merely enhance them.

SUGGESTIONS FOR
FURTHER READING

The following short list of books consists of a few works which the editors have found interesting and useful. There are literally thousands of printed works which deal primarily with Oxford, many of which are for the expert. The ones listed here are for the pleasure of the traveller who would like to read a few more things about, or set in, Oxford. The second part of the list consists of only a few of the many hundreds of novels about Oxford that are available.

Beadle, Muriel. *These Ruins are Inhabited*. Garden City, New York: Doubleday, 1961.

Brittain, Vera. *The Women at Oxford*. London: Harrap, 1960.

Green, Vivian H. H. *A History of Oxford University*. London: Batsford, 1974.

Lobel, Mary D., and Salter, H.A. *The Victoria History of the County of Oxford*, vol 3, *The University of Oxford*. This monumental project, begun in 1907 by the University of London, issued this particular volume in 1954.

Mason, Mercia. *Blue Guide: Oxford and Cambridge* (third edition). London and New York: A & C. Black and W. W. Norton, 1987.

Morris, Jan. *The Oxford Book of Oxford*. Oxford: Oxford University Press, 1978.

Sutcliffe, Peter. *The Oxford University Press, An Informal History*. Oxford: Oxford University Press, 1978.

Thomas, J. W. *Oxford: The Golden Heart of Britain*. Oxford: Thomas-Photo, distributed by Basil Blackwell, n.d. A very nice picture book.

Woolley, A. R. *The Clarendon Guide to Oxford* (fifth edition). Oxford: Oxford University Press, 1983.

NOVELS

Beerbohm, Max. *Zuleika Dobson*. New York: Signet Classic, 1966 (first published in 1911). An incomparably witty fantasy about Oxford life at the turn of the century, set in Judas College.

Sayers, Dorothy. *Gaudy Night*. New York: Avon Books, 1968 (originally published in 1935). One of the very best of the many detective stories set in Oxford, this one at a women's College called Shrewsbury.

Stewart, J. I. M. *The Oxford Quintet*. Includes *The Gaudy, Young Pattullo, A Memorial Service, The Madonna of the Astrolabe*, and *Full Term*. Published originally by Gollancz from 1974-78.

Most of these and many other Oxford novels are available in paperback from various publishers.

A

Pocket Companion

FOR

OXFORD.

CONTAINING,

An Accurate Defcription of the PUBLIC EDIFICES,
the BUILDINGS in each of the COLLEGES, the
GARDENS, STATUES, BUSTS, PICTURES,
the HIEROGLYPHICKS at MAGDALEN COL-
LEGE, and all other CURIOSITIES, in the
UNIVERSITY. With an Hiftorical Account
of the Foundation of the Colleges, their Hiftory, and prefent State.

To which is prefix'd,

Correct LISTS of the CHANCELLORS, HIGH-STEW
ARDS, VICE-CHANCELLORS, PROFESSORS, LEC-
TURERS, &c.

WITH

Perfpective VIEWS of RADCLIFFE'S LIBRARY, MAG-
DALEN COLLEGE NEW BUILDING, NEW COLLEGE
from the Garden, PECKWATER SQUARE, and the
inner Quadrangle of ALL-SOUL'S COLLEGE.

A new EDITION, with ADDITIONS.

OXFORD:

Printed for R. CLEMENTS, near the *Theatre* ; and Sold
by R. BALDWIN, in *Pater nofter-Row*, London, 1756.

See! *Oxford* lifts her Head fublime,
Majeftic in the Mofs of Time;
Nor wants there *Græcia*'s better Part,
'Mid the proud Piles of antient Art;
Nor decent Doric to difpenfe
New Charms 'mid old Magnificence;
And here and there foft Corinth weaves
Her dædal Coronet of Leaves;
While, as with rival Pride, her Tow'rs invade
the Sky.

WARTON's Ode.[1]

CONTENTS.

COLLEGES *and* HALLS.

A.

Jesus

LIST

L I S T

O F

Late and prefent Chancellors, High-Stewards, Vice-Chancellors; and prefent Reprefentatives in Parliament, Proctors, Profeffors, Lecturers, &c. &c.

CHANCELLORS.

1688. James Duke of Ormond.
1715. Charles Earl of Arran.

HIGH-STEWARDS.

1711. Henry Earl of Clarendon and Rochefter.
1754. John Earl of Weftmoreland.

VICE-CHANCELLORS.

1750. Rev. John Browne, D. D. Mafter of Univerfity College.
1754. Rev. George Huddesford, D. D. Prefident of Trinity College.

REPRESENTATIVES in PARLIAMENT.

Sir Roger Newdigate, Bart.
Peregrine Palmer, Efq;

Proctors,

Proctors, an Annual Office, taken from the Colleges, according to the following Table.

1.	Christ-Church and	St. John's Colleges.
2.	Magdalen ———	New Coll.
3.	Merton ———	Brazenose.
4.	Christ-Church ———	All-Souls.
5.	Corpus Christi———	Exeter.
6.	Magdalen ———	Wadham.
7.	St. John's ———	Queen's.
8.	Christ-Church ———	New Coll.
9.	Trinity ———	Oriel.
10.	Magdalen ———	Merton.
11.	Christ Church———	Brazenose.
12.	All-Souls ———	Lincoln.
13.	Exeter ———	University.
14.	New College ———	Wadham.
15.	Magdalen ———	Christ-Church
16.	St. John's ———	Merton.
17.	Corpus Christi———	Balioll.
18.	Brazenose ———	Oriel.
19.	Christ-Church———	Magdalen.
20.	New College ———	All-Souls.
21.	Exeter ———	Queen's.
22.	Trinity ———	Wadham.
23.	Jesus ———	Pembroke.

Regius Professor of Divinity.
Rev. John Fanshawe, D. D. Canon of Christ-Church.

Margaret Professor of Divinity.
Rev. Thomas Jenner, D. D. President of Magdalen College

Regius Professor of Hebrew.
Rev. Tho. Hunt, D. D. Canon of Christ-Church.
Regius

Regius Profeſſor of Greek.
Rev. Samuel Dickens, D. D. of Chriſt-Church.

Regius Profeſſor of Civil Law.
Robert Jenner, D. C. L. of Trinity College.

Regius Profeſſor of Phyſick.
William Woodforde, M. D. of New College.

Regius Profeſſor of Modern Languages.
Rev. Joſeph Spence, A. M. of New College.

Savilian Profeſſor of Aſtronomy.
Rev. James Bradley, D. D. and King's Profeſſor
of Aſtronomy, of Baliol College.

Savilian Profeſſor of Geometry.
Rev. Nathaniel Bliſs, A. M. of Pemb. Coll.

Profeſſor of Natural Philoſophy.
Rev. Joſeph Browne, D. D. of Queen's Coll.

Profeſſor of Moral Philoſophy.
George Smyth, A. M. of New College.

Profeſſor of Hiſtory.
Richard Frewin, M. D. of Chriſt-Church.

Profeſſor of Chemiſtry.

────────   ────────   ────────

Profeſſor of Anatomy.
Thomas Lawrence, M. D. of Trinity College.

Profeſſor of Botany.
Humphrey Sibthorpe, M. D. of Magd. College.

Archbiſhop Laud's Profeſſor of Arabick.
Rev. Thomas Hunt, D. D. Canon of Ch. Ch.

Lord

Lord Almoner's Professor of Arabic.
Rev. Richard Browne, D. D. of Trinity Coll.

Professor of Musick.
William Hayes, Doctor of Musick, of Magd. Coll.

Professor of Poetry.
William Hawkins, A. M. of Pembroke College.

Publick Orator.
Rev. Roger Mather, A. M. of Brazenose Coll.

Keeper of the Archives.
Rev. Francis Wise, B. D. of Trinity Coll.

Keeper of the Ashmole Musæum.
William Huddesford, B. A. of Trinity College.

Register of the University.
Henry Fisher, A. M. of Jesus College.

Publick Librarian.
Rev. Humphrey Owen, B. D. of Jesus College.

Keeper of Radcliffe's Library.
Rev. Francis Wise, B. D. of Trinity College.

University Officers.

Robt Eyton, A. M. of Physic and Arts,
William Walker, A. M. of Divinity,
Herbert Beaver, A. M. of Law,
} *Esquire Beadles.*

Mr. Wm. Sherwin, of Physic and Arts,
Mr. John Pottle, of Divinity,
Mr. Samuel Parker, of Law,
} *Yeomen Beadles.*

Mr. Henry Church, *Virger.*

THE

THE

Gentleman *and* Lady's

POCKET COMPANION

FOR

O X F O R D.

General *DESCRIPTION.*

*O*XFORD appears from ancient Records to have been a confiderable Place even in the Time of the *Romans*; and to have been called *Bellofitum.* We learn alfo, that before their Conquefts, the *Britains* confecrated it to the Mufes, whom they tranfplanted hither, as to a more fertile Nurfery, from *Creeklade* in *Wiltſhire.* Before King *Alfred's* Time[2], whofe Reign began A. D. 872. *Thomas Rudburn*, Biſhop of *Cheſter*, calls it an *Univerſity* in his *Chronicon Hydenſe:* So that *Alfred* was only the Reſtorer of Learning. Before the Conqueſt, there was a College built, where *Robert D'Oylie* afterwards built the Caſtle (A. D. 1071.) in which was a Prior or Dean, and fome Secular, who became afterwards regular Canons. In A. D.

1129,

1129, the said College was translated to *Osney* Abby, by *Robert D'Oylie*, Nephew to the former, who erected it into a Bishop's See, called the Bishopric of *Oxford*; translated A. D. 1546. to St. *Fridefwide*'s Monastry, now called *Christ-Church*.[3]

King *Henry* I. built a Royal Palace in *Beaumont*, near *Gloucester-Green*; the Ruins of which are still visible.[4] King *Richard* I. surnamed *Cœur de Lion*, was born here. Archbishop *Usher* affirms, that in King *Henry* the Third's Time, 30,000 Students resided here: and *Rishanger* (who lived in the same Reign, which continued 58 Years) says, that notwithstanding the Civil Wars had so much disturbed the Peace and Quiet of this venerable Seat of Learning, yet, in his Time, there was remaining 15000 Students, whose Names were entered in the Matriculation Book. About which Time, *John Baliol* (Father of *Baliol*, King of *Scots*) built a College, now called by his Name, A. D. 1269: And *Walter de Merton* Bishop of *Rochester*, that which is now called *Merton* College; both of them beautified with Buildings, and enriched with Lands; and were the first endowed Colleges in Christendom. King *Alfred* built three Colleges in it; one for Divinity, another for Philosophy, and a third for Grammar. Soon afterwards the *Danes* burnt it, and *Harold Harefoot*, who reign'd in 1036, to revenge the Death of some of his Followers slain here, so violently treated them, that the Scholars left it, and it lay waste till about the *Norman* Conquest. In the Time of King *John* the Students being badly us'd by the Townsmen, went part to *Reading* and part to *Cambridge*. After these Matters were again settled, the Students divided into two Factions, the North and the South; in Discontent the latter left *Oxford*, and went to *Stamford* in *Lincolnshire*, where
they

they began to erect an University; but when this Quarrel was adjusted, they return'd, and have continu'd here ever since. *Semper floreant Academiæ!*

It is situated on a small Eminence, rising gradually from its Extremities to the Center. It is encompassed by Meadows and Corn Fields. The Meadows, which are chiefly to the South and West, are about a Mile over; beyond which are Hills of a moderate Height, bounding the Prospect.

The Eastern Prospect is likewise bounded by Hills at a moderate Distance; the Valley growing considerably narrower towards the South: But the North is open to Corn-fields and Enclosures for many Miles together, without an Hill to intercept the free Current of Air which purifies it from all noxious Vapours. It is washed by a great Number of plenteous Streams: On the East, by the different Branches of the *Cherwell*; on the South and West, by those of the *Isis*; all which meet and join Hands a little below the City, forming one beautiful River. The Soil is dry, being on a fine Gravel. Upon the whole, it is as healthful and pleasant a Spot as any in the Kingdom.

The whole Town, including the Suburbs, is a Mile in Length from East to West, and almost as much in Breadth from North to South; being three Miles in Circumference: but it is of an irregular Figure, and many void Spaces are comprehended within these Limits, besides the numerous Courts and Gardens belonging to the respective Colleges.

The City, properly so called, formerly surrounded by an embattled Wall, with Bastions at about 150 Feet Distance from each other; is of an oblong Form, and not much more than two Miles in Circumference.

cumference. *Magdalen College*, with the Eastern
as well as Northern Suburbs, which contain the
Parishes of *Holy-well*, *Magdalen*, St. *Clement*'s, and
St. *Giles*'s, with *Baliol*, *Trinity*, St. *John*'s and
Wadham Colleges, are without the old Walls, of
which a confiderable Part remains as a Boundary
to *New College*; beginning near *Eaft-Gate*, and
continuing almoft to the *Clarendon* Printing-houfe,
where there was a Portal and a Chapel; fome Remains of which are ftill vifible: Likewife from *Eaft-
Gate* Southwards, almoft to *Chrift-Church*, making
an entire boundary to the Eaft and South Sides of
Merton College. The Fortifications and Outworks,
raifed by the *Royalifts* in the Time of the Civil
Wars, included all the Suburbs; but they are now
almoft entirely demolifhed.[6]

The principal Street of the City runs from Eaft
to Weft, almoft the Length of the Town, but under different Names; the *High-Street*, beginning
at the *Eaft-Gate*, includes at leaft two Thirds of
that Length; the Remainder is called the *Old Butcher-Row*, and *Caftle-Street*.[7] The *High-Street* is
perhaps without a Rival; being of a fpacious Width
and Length, clean and well paved, adorned with
the Fronts of three well built Colleges; St. *Mary*'s
and *All-Saints* Churches; before the former an
handfome new built Stone Wall and a broad Pavement, (now called the Parade) the latter with a Parapet Wall and Iron Palifades; terminated at one
End by the Conduit and *Carfax* Church, and at the
other by *Eaft-Gate*, and a View of *Magdalen* College Tower. Some objeét to its not being ftrait;
but others think that a Beauty: For ev'ry Turn of
it prefents a new Objeét, and a different View;
each of which would make an agreeable Piéture in
Perfpeétive: Whereas, had it been ftrait, every
                                              Objeét

Object would have been seen at one and the same Instant, but more fore-shortened and eclipsed than at present.

The second Street in *Oxford* is that which runs from South to North, crossing the Street already described, from whence that Part of the Town has obtained the Name of *Quater Vois*, or the Four Ways, corruptly called *Carfax*; as the Corporation Church, which stands near the Four Ways, likewise is.[8]

The South End of this second Street is call'd *Fish-Street*, and the other End of it the *Corn-Market*; from whence we pass through *Bocardo*, or the North Gate, into *Magdalen* Parish, and St. *Giles's*, which form a very spacious Street, and in some respects is preferable to either of the former, especially to such as love Retirement; it having the Pleasure and Advantage of the Country, tho' connected with the Town. It hath much the appearance of a neat Country Village; being well planted with Elms, the Houses (many of which are built of hewn Stone) having for the most part Grass-plots before them, and Gardens or Corn-Fields behind them. One End of this Street is handsomely terminated by St. *Giles's* Church; and the other by *Magdalen* Church: tho' somewhat eclipsed by the middle Row of Houses. This Street is likewise adorned with the Front of St. *John's* College.

On the East Side of *Fish-Street* (commonly called St. *Tole's*, by Corruption from St. *Aldate's*, which Parish includes the greatest Part of this Street) stands *Christ-Church* College; the magnificent Front whereof extends 382 Feet.[9] Also the TOWN-HALL where the Town and County Sessions, and the Assizes are held; which is newly rebuilt in an elegant Taste, with all Manner of Con-

veniencies for the separate Courts, *viz.* Rooms for
the Grand and Petty Juries, &c. with an Arcade
underneath, at the Expence of that worthy Patri-
ot and Citizen THOMAS ROWNEY, Esq; one of
the present Representatives in Parliament, and
High Steward of this City.[10]

The chief Bridges are, first, the East (commonly called *Maudlin*) Bridge over the *Cherwell*; this
extends 678 Feet, and consists of 20 Stone Arches.
It was first built by *Robert D'Oylie*, who built the
Castle as abovementioned; but it has been considerably widened within these Thirty Years. This
is the Grand Entrance from *London*. The second,
on the South Side of the Town, is over the *Isis*;
where there is a Gate commonly called Friar *Bacon's*
Study.[11] This is the Entrance from *Abingdon* in
Berks, and is itself also in that County. The third,
on the West Side, is likewise over the *Isis*, and is
called *High-bridge*; from hence runs a Causey of a
Mile in Length, across the Meadows abovementioned, which consists partly of *Terra firma*, and partly of Stone Bridges over the different Branches of
the *Isis*: One in particular near the Middle thereof,
viz. Bulstock Bridge, is over the navigable Stream
which comes from *Letchlade* in *Gloucestershire*.

There are in the City of *Oxford*, and Liberties,
thirteen Parishes, *viz.* 1. St. *Mary's*. 2. *All-
Saints*. 3. St. *Martin's*, or *Carfax*. 4. St. *Aldate's*, or St. *Tole's*. 5. St. *Ebb's*. 6. St. *Peter's*
in the *Bayly*. 7. St. *Michael's*. 8. St. *Mary Magdalen*. 9. St. *Peter* in the East. 10. *Holywell*.
11. St. *Giles's*. 12. St. *Thomas's*, and 13. St.
John's.

Of the Churches which give Names to the several Parishes already enumerated, there are but
four which are remarkable, *viz.* St. *Mary's*, *All-
Saints*,

Saints, St. *Peter*'s in the East, and St. *John*'s.[12] St.
Mary's stands on the North Side of the *High-Street*,
and is the Church to which the University resort on
Sundays and Holidays to hear Sermons preached by
the Appointment of the Vice-Chancellor; and the
Parishioners, at different Times of the Day, attend
Divine Service here. It is a well-proportioned
Church, and handsomely built, tho' Gothic. The
Porch, indeed, is in a more modern Taste; it was
built at the Expence of Dr. *Morgan Owen*, Chaplain to Archbishop *Laud*, A. D. 1637. and cost
230 *l.* The Church consists of three Isles, and a
large Chancel, which is paved with black and white
Marble. The *Vice-Chancellor* sits at the West End
of the middle Isle, on a kind of Throne elevated
some few Steps; a little below sit the two Proctors;
on either Hand, descending, the Heads of Houses
and Doctors; below these, the young Noblemen;
and in the Area, on Benches, the Masters of Arts.
At the West End, with a Return to the North and
South Isles, are Galleries for Bachelors and Undergraduates; and under the middle one are Seats for
the Wives and Daughters of the Heads of Houses,
and female Strangers of Distinction. Adjoining
to the North Isle, is *Adam de Brome*'s Chapel;
where the *Vice-Chancellor*, Heads of Houses, Proctors and Preacher assemble before Sermon, and
from thence go in Procession to their respective
Places. The Pulpit stands in the Center of the
middle Isle. In the Arch between the Church and
Chancel, stands a good Organ, originally built by
Father *Smith*, and since improved by Mr. *John
Byfield*. This is not the first Organ erected in this
Church; for *W. Gray*, Archdeacon of *Berkshire*,
dying A. D. 1521. bequeath'd four Pounds to buy
a *new Pair of Organs*, to be *play'd upon* in it. The
Tower

Tower and Spire, which rises from the Ground to the perpendicular Height of 180 Feet, is a very noble Structure, and contains a Ring of Six heavy Bells. In Term Time, one or other of these is toll'd or rung out, to give notice of a *Convocation* or *Congregation*, and the Performance of the University Exercises.[13]

On the Left-side of the West Window, next to the *High-Street*, is a pretty Piece of Sculpture, representing a Woman down to the Waist: It is well designed, and properly executed; though Time or Accident hath somewhat impaired the Face, which has been beautiful. The Hood is of modern Fashion. It is remarkable that Foreigners compliment this Curiosity with their Notice, tho' little observed by the Inhabitants.

All-Saints Church stands in the same Street, a little to the Westward of St. *Mary*'s; and is a very beautiful Fabric of white hewn Stone. It is adorned, both within and without, with Pilasters of the Corinthian Order, an *Attic* Story and Balustrade elegantly finishing it without, a curious fretwork Cieling, a neat Altar-Piece, Pulpit, Marble Font, and regular Pews within. This Church is 72 Feet long, 42 wide, and 50 high, without a Pillar.

The Steeple is built after the Manner of some of the new Churches in *London*. The Architect, the Rev. Dr. *Aldrich*, formerly Dean of *Christ-Church*.

St. *Peter*'s in the East, standing backwards from the above Street, nigh unto *Queen's-College*, is near 800 Years old; and was the first Church built of Stone in this Part of the Kingdom. It is in good Condition, and likely to stand as many Years longer. It was formerly the University Church; and even now, the University go to it every *Sunday* in
the

the Afternoon during Lent. This Parish has more to boast of, perhaps, (exclusive of what has been mentioned) than any one in *Europe* beside: For it contains five Colleges; *viz. University, Queens, New-College, Magdalen,* and *Hertford* Colleges; three Halls; *viz.* St. *Edmund, Magdalen,* and *Alban* Halls; Two Peals of Ten Bells, and one of Six; and three Organs: Two of which belong to Chapels, where Cathedral Service is performed twice a Day, and the other, to the Mother-Church.

The last Church which deserves Attention, is that of St. *John*'s; which is a handsome Gothic Building: But for further Particulars, we refer our Reader to *Merton* College; to which it seems more connected at present than to the Parish.

There is little left of the Castle except a square Tower, and some broken Walls of immense Thickness.

Near the Castle are the Ruins of the ancient Town-Hall, where, in 1577, was held the Black Affize, when the Lieutenant of the County, eight Esquires and Justices, and almost all the Gentlemen of the grand Jury, died of the poisonous Smell from the Jail. Above One Hundred Scholars, besides Townsmen, were seiz'd with the Distemper. It lasted about a Month, when the Infection ceas'd. On the Top of the artificial Hill, near the Castle, is an entry into a large arch'd Room, formerly us'd as a Magazine in Time of War. Not far from hence is a pleasant Garden, called *Paradise,* formerly much frequented; but of late taken little notice of.

The UNIVERSITY LIBRARY, usually called the *Bodleian,* from Sir *Thomas Bodley,* its principal
Founder.

Founder. This is a large, lofty Structure, built
of Stone, in the Form of a *Roman* H, and is said to
contain the greatest Number of Books of any Library in *Europe*, (except that of the *Vatican*) a Catalogue whereof is printed, being itself two Folios
of no mean Size.

To give some Account of the Foundation of the
public Library from *Campden*. ' The Ground on
' which the Divinity School was built was pur-
' chased by the University in the Year 1427, and
' upon several Contributions that Structure was
' soon after begun, but intermitted, till, by the
' Piety of *Humphrey* Duke of *Glocester*, it was car-
' ried on and compleated.' This is esteemed a most
elegant Piece of Gothic Architecture, surpassing
every Thing of the Kind in the University; being
well proportioned, and finished in the highest
Taste; especially its Roof. ' The same Duke,
' over the Divinity School, erected this Library,
' which he furnished with 129 choice Volumes he
' procured from *Italy*; besides which he gave 126
' Volumes more in the Year 1440, and in the Year
' 1443 a much greater Number, besides consider-
' able Additions at his Death, three Years after:'
But these Books have been long since lost.

In the Year 1597, Sir *Thomas Bodley*, Knt. formerly a Member of this University, repaired the
old Library of *Humphrey* Duke of *Glocester*, and
fitted it for the Reception of Books, *A. D.* 1599.
An additional Eastern Gallery was begun by him in
the Year 1610, and another Gallery, projected by
him, was erected afterwards.

Sir *Thomas Bodley* furnished the Library with the
best Books he could procure from all Parts of the
World, in Memory of which Benefaction, the
Earl

Earl of *Dorset* caused the Statue of Sir *Thomas* to be erected in the Library.

Sir *Thomas Bodley* died *Jan.* 28, 1612, leaving a considerable Estate in Land and Money for Salaries to the Officers, and keeping the Library in Repair. He also left Statutes for the Government of it, which were confirmed in Convocation; and Sir *Thomas* was declared by the University to be the Founder.

The Earl of *Pembroke* afterwards, by the Persuasion of Archbishop *Laud*, gave almost all the Collection of *Greek* Manuscripts, which *Francis Barroccio* the *Venetian* had gathered together with great Pains and Cost, thought to be the most valuable Collection that ever came into *England* at once. The Earl reserved 22 of them for his own Use, which *Cromwell* bought, and gave afterwards; and Sir *Thomas Roe* added another choice Parcel of *Greek* Manuscripts.

Sir *Kenelm Digby* also presented a great Number of Manuscripts, new bound, which he had gotten in his Travels; and Archbishop *Laud* having sent into the East to buy Oriental Manuscripts, and to the Marts in *Germany*, procured thirteen hundred large Volumes of Books, written in above twenty Languages. By this Bishop's Instigation the University added another Building to Duke *Humphrey*'s Library, which brought it into the Shape of a *Roman* H, where, besides the Books before mention'd, the most excellent Study of the Learned *John Selden*, of the *Inner-Temple*, *London*, Esq; is placed. Underneath this additional Side of the Library, is the Convocation House; in the Apodyterium of which the Vice-Chancellor's Court is held. Many other Benefactors have much increased this Library; General *Fairfax*, afterwards Lord *Fairfax*; Dr.

2　　　　　　　　　　　　　　　　*Marshall*,

Marſhall, Rector of *Lincoln* College; Dr. *Barlow*, late Lord Biſhop of *Lincoln*, &c. which, with certain Libraries purchaſed by the Univerſity of Dr. *Huntingdon*, Mr. *Greaves*, and Dr. *Pocock*, have made it the largeſt Univerſity Library in *Europe*.

The Buildings adjoining are the PUBLIC SCHOOLS, which, with one Side of the Library, form a ſmall Square of 105 Feet over either Way. The principal Front of the Schools on the Outſide is about 175 Feet in Length, in the Middle whereof is a great Gate, with a magnificent Tower over it, in which is Sir *Henry Saville*'s Library; and the higheſt Apartments of the Tower are uſed for Aſtronomical Obſervations, and ſome Experiments in Philoſophy; and from thence called the Obſervatory. Three Sides of the upper Story of the SCHOOLS are one entire Room, and called the PICTURE GALLERY. It is furniſhed with the Pourtraits of many learned and famous Men, ſeveral large Cabinets of Medals, and ſome Caſes of Books; being intended as a Continuation to the *Bodleian* Library. Dr. *Tanner*, the late Biſhop of St. *Aſaph*, bequeathing his valuable Collection of Manuſcripts to the Univerſity, together with a Sum of Money to erect proper Caſes for them, they are here depoſited, near the Entrance into the Gallery.

Dr. *Edward Butler*, late Preſident of *Magdalen* College, bequeathed the Sum of 200 *l.* to carry on the Wainſcotting of the ſame; which Scheme the preſent moſt noble Duke of BEAUFORT, in the Year 1749, approving, ordered it to be completely finiſhed at his Expence, as a teſtimony of his ſincere Affection for the Place where his Grace received his Education. This being now done, and the

Pictures

Pictures cleaned and repaired by Mr. *Crawford*, they are, by the great Pains and Judgment of the present worthy Librarian, more advantageously disposed than heretofore; and their Number greatly increased by late Benefactions. The Arundelian Marbles are now placed to great Advantage in the Moral Philosophy School.

Near the Schools stands the THEATRE, in Form almost of a *Roman* D, only longer in Proportion from Right to Left; it hath a flat Roof, composed of short Pieces of Timber, continued to a great Breadth, without Arch-work or Pillar to support them, being sustained only by the Side-Walls and their own Texture, tho' from Side-Wall to Side-Wall it is 80 Feet over one Way, and 70 the other; which gave Occasion to say, that the Foundation was on the Roof.

When properly filled, the Vice-Chancellor being seated in the Center of the semicircular Part, the Doctors on his Right and Left Hand, the Proctors and Curators in their Robes, the Masters of Arts, Bachelors, and Under-Graduates, in their respective Habits and Places, together with Strangers of both Sexes, it makes the most august Appearance of any Room whatever.

Mr. *Hogarth*, when here at the Opening of the *Radcliffe* Library, furnished himself with Materials for two different Views of it; and it were greatly to be wished, he would oblige the World by putting them in Execution.

On the Outside it is adorned with Sculpture; particularly the Statues of *Charles* II. the old Duke of *Ormond*, and Archbishop *Sheldon*; done by *Chair*: Within, with Painting, *viz.* the Pourtraits, at full Length, of the Founder Archbishop

C

Sheldon,

Sheldon, the fame Duke of *Ormond*, and Sir *Chri-*
stopher Wren the Architect: Likewife a curious
Cieling; of which the following is a Defcription.

In Imitation of the Theatres of the ancient
Greeks and *Romans*, which were too large to be
cover'd with Lead or Tile, fo this, by the Painting of the flat Roof within, is reprefented open;
and as they ftretched a Cordage from Pilafter to
Pilafter, upon which they ftrain'd a Covering of
Cloth, to protect the People from the Injuries of
the Weather, fo here is a Cord-moulding gilded,
that reaches crofs and crofs the Houfe, both in
Length and Breadth, which fupporteth a great
Reddifh Drapery, fuppos'd to have covered the
Roof, but now furl'd up by the *Genii* round a-
bout the Houfe, toward the Wall, which difco-
vereth the open Air, and maketh Way for the
Defcent of the *Arts* and *Sciences*, that are congre-
gated in a Circle of Clouds, to whofe Affembly
Truth defcends, as being follicited and implor'd by
them all.

For Joy of this Feftival fome other *Genii* fport
about the Clouds, with their Feftoons of Flowers
and Lawrels, and prepare their Garlands of Lawrels and Rofes, *viz. Honour* and *Pleafure*, for the
great Lovers and Students of thofe Arts: And that
this Affembly might be perfectly happy, their great
Enemies and Difturbers, *Envy, Rapine*, and *Bru-
tality*, are by the *Genii* of their oppofite Virtues,
viz. Prudence, Fortitude, and *Eloquence*, driven
from the Society, and thrown down Head-long
from the Clouds: The Report of the Affembly of
the one, and the Expulfion of the other, being
proclaim'd thro' the open and ferene Air, by fome
other

other of the *Genii*, who blowing their antick Trumpets, divide themfelves into the feveral Quarters of the World.

Hitherto in Grofs.

More particularly the Circle of Figures confift, Firft of *Theology*, with her Book of Seven Seals, imploring the Affiftance of *Truth* for the unfolding of it.

On her Left-hand is the *Mofaical Law* vailed, with the Tables of Stone, to which fhe points with her Iron Rod.

On her Right-hand is the *Gofpel*, with the Crofs in one Hand, and a Chalice in the other.

In the fame Divifion, over the *Mofaical Law*, is *Hiftory*, holding up her Pen, as dedicating it to *Truth*, and an attending *Genius*, with feveral Fragments of Old Writing, from which fhe collects her Hiftory into her Book.

On the other Side, near the *Gofpel*, is *Divine Poefy*, with her Harp of *David*'s Fafhion.

In the Triangle on the Right-hand of the *Gofpel*, is alfo *Logick*, in a Pofture of arguing; and on the Left-hand of the *Mofaical Law*, is *Mufick*, with her Antick Lyre, having a Pen in her Hand, and a Paper of Mufick Notes on her Knee, with a *Genius* on her Right-hand, (a little within the Partition of *Theology*) playing on a Flute, being the Emblem of ancient Mufick.

On the Left (but within the Partition for *Phyfick*) *Dramatick Poefy*, with a Vizard, reprefenting *Comedy*, a bloody Dagger for *Tragedy*, and the Reed Pipe for *Paftoral*.

In the Square on the Right Side of the Circle, is *Law*, with her Ruling Scepter, accompanied with Records, Patents, and Evidences on the one

Side, and on the other with *Rhetorick:* By thefe is an attending *Genius*, with the Scales of *Juftice*, and a Figure with a Palm-branch, the Emblem of Reward for virtuous Actions; and the *Roman Fafces*, the Marks of Power and Punifhment.

Printing, with a Cafe of Letters in one Hand, and a Form ready fet in the other, and by her feveral Sheets hanging as a drying.

On the Left Side the Circle, oppofite to *Theology*, in three Squares, are the *Mathematical Sciences*, (depending on *Demonftration*, as the other on *Faith*) in the firft of which is *Aftronomy* with the Celeftial Globe, *Geography* with the Terreftrial, together with three attending *Genii*; having *Arithmetick* in the Square on one Hand, with a Paper of Figures; *Optics* with the Perfpective-Glafs; *Geometry* with a Pair of Compaffes in her Left; and a Table with *Geometrical* Figures in it, in her Right-Hand. And in the Square on the other Hand, *Architecture* embracing the Capital of a Column, with Compaffes, and the Norma or Square lying by her, and a Workman holding another Square in one Hand, and a Plumb-Line in the other.

In the midft of thefe Squares and Triangles (as defcending from above) is the Figure of *Truth* fitting as on a Cloud, in one Hand holding a Palm Branch (the Emblem of Victory) in the other the Sun, whofe Brightnefs enlightens the whole Circle of Figures, and is fo bright, that it feems to hide the Face of herfelf to the Spectators below.

Over the Entrance of the Front of the THE-ATRE, are Three Figures tumbling down; Firft *Envy*, with her Snaky Hairs, Squint Eyes, Hag's Breaft, pale venomous Complexion, ftrong, but ugly Limbs, and rivel'd Skin, frighted from above by
the

the Sight of the Shield of *Pallas*, with the *Gorgon's* Head in it, against which she opposes her snaky Tresses, but her Fall is so precipitous, that she has no Command of her Arms.

Then *Rapine*, with her fiery Eyes, grinning Teeth, sharp Twangs, her Hands imbrued in Blood, holding a bloody Dagger in one Hand, in the other a burning Flambeau; with these Instruments threatening the Destruction of Learning, and all its Habitations, but is overcome, and prevented, by a *Herculean Genius*, or Power.

Next that is represented brutish, scoffing Ignorance, endeavouring to vilify and contemn what she understands not, which is charmed by a *mercurial Genius* with his *Caduceus*.

In the Theatre are held the Public Acts, called the *Comitia*, or *Encænia*: At which solemn Times there are several extraordinary Proctors appointed, who are to take Care that public Peace is observed, and that all Persons are placed according to their Degrees.

This Edifice, which justly deserves to be deemed one of our principal Curiosities, was built by that celebrated Architect Sir *Christopher Wren*, at the Expence of Archbishop *Sheldon*, the Chancellor, A.D. 1669, and cost his Grace no less than 15000l. besides which, he left 2000 l. to purchase Lands for the perpetual Repair of it.

On the West of the Theatre stands *Ashmole's* MUSÆUM, a handsome Edifice, built by the University, of white hewn Stone, in the Form of our modern Houses, being about 60 Feet long.[14] It was finished in the Year 1683, when a very valuable Collection of Antiquities and foreign Curiosities

were

were prefented to the Univerfity, and repofited in
it, by *Elias Afhmole*, Efq; this Infcription being
fet upon the Front of the Building, next to the
Street, viz.

*Mufæum Afhmoleanum, Schola Naturalis Hiflo-
riæ, Officina Chymica.*

But the grand Entrance is at that End which is
nearest to the Theatre, and oppofite to one of the
Entrances into it. It is a beautiful Portico in the
Corinthian Order, and very richly embellifhed
with Sculpture: Befide which, there are Feftoons
and other Decorations properly adapted to the Purpofe it was built for; fuch as Shells, Snakes, Cro-
cadiles, &c.

Among many other Benefactions, Dr. *Huntington* added fome *Egyptian* Hieroglyphics and other
Antiquities; Mr. *Aaron Goodear* an entire Mum-
my; Dr. *Martin Lifler* a large Cabinet of natural
Curiofities of his own collecting, and feveral *Roman* Antiquities ; Dr. *Pound* a numerous Collection of Plants and Animals, brought by him from
China, and preferved in Spirits ; the whole making
one of the richeft Repofitories of Curiofities in
Europe.

An excellent Collection of Manufcripts, collect-
ed by Mr. *Afhmole* and his Father Sir *W. Dugdale*,
is here repofited ; as is likewife Mr. *Anthony à
Wood*'s Library.

In a Room on the firft Floor, Dr. *Bradley* reads his
Courfe of Lectures in Experimental Philofophy ; and
in the lower Part of the Building is the Elaboratory,
where Lectures are read in Chymiftry and Anatomy.[15]
This alfo was built by Sir *Chriflopher Wren.*

On the other Side of the Theatre, and North of
the Schools, ftands the *Clarendon* PRINTING-
HOUSE,

HOUSE, built in the Year 1711, with the Profits arising from the Sale of Lord *Clarendon*'s History; the Copy of which was given to the University by the Lords *Clarendon* and *Rochester*, Sons of that noble Lord.[16] It is a grand Edifice, 115 Feet in Length; and consists of two lofty Stories built with white hewn Stone and sashed. Towards the Street, it has a magnificent *Portico* in the *Doric* Order; the height of the Columns being equal to the two Stories: This is answered on the opposite Side, next the Schools, by a Frontispiece supported by Three-Quarter Columns of the same Dimensions; and the Doric Entablature encompasses the whole Building. On the Top, are Statues of the nine Muses; and over the Entrance on the South Side a Statue of the Earl of *Clarendon*. As we enter on this Side, on the Right Hand are Printing-Rooms, where Bibles and Common-Prayer Books are printed: Over which is a very grand Apartment, most elegantly furnished; and, underneath, a Kitchen and all other Conveniencies for a Family: For which, Mr. *Basket*, the King's Printer, pays a considerable Rent to the University.

On the Left-hand is the University Press; where Books in all Sciences and Languages are printed. Besides the Apartments assigned for the Press-Men, Compositors, and Store-Keeper, there is one with a Lobby or Anti-Chamber reserved for the Heads of Houses and Delegates to meet in; which is well proportioned and finely finished: In this Room is a very good Picture of Queen *Ann* by Sir *Godfrey Kneller*.

Southward of the Schools, in the Center of a beautiful *Area*, adorned with a considerable Number of Obelisks and Lamps, stands the new public Library;

brary; for the building whereof, that celebrated
Phyſician Dr. *John Radcliffe* bequeathed the Sum
of 40,000 *l*. He fixed the Sallary of the Librarian
at 150 *l. per Annum*; appropriated 100 *l. per Annum*
to buy Books, and 100 *l. per Annum* to keep the
ſaid Library in Repair.

The Ruſtic Baſement, which is 100 Feet in Diameter from Outſide to Outſide, is a double Octo-
gon or 16 Square; eight of which Squares are di-
ſtinguiſhed by their Projection, and having over
each a Pediment or Frontiſpiece that forms them
into Gate-ways.

The Superſtructure, raiſed upon this Baſement,
is perfectly *Cylindrical*, and adorned with Three-
Quarter Columns of the *Corinthian* Order; which
are ranged, not at equal Diſtances, but in Coup-
lets.   Between theſe, there is an Alternacy of Windows and Niches all round: Over the latter, next
to the *Architrave*, are beautiful Feſtoons of Fruits
and Flowers.   The Entablature is much enriched
with Carving; and over it is a Balluſtrade ſurround-
ing the whole, finiſhed with Vaſes on the Piers perpendicular to the Columns.   This is at the height
of 80 Feet; above which, tho' conſiderably con-
tracted, is a Cupola of 60; the Manner in which
it is built may better be comprehended by a Glance
at the Print annexed, than from the moſt accurate
verbal Deſcription; to which, therefore, we refer
the Reader, and proceed to give ſome Account of
the Inſide.   Seven of the Gate-ways abovementioned are Entrances into the *Portico* or *Arcade*; in
the Center of which within the Piers is a wide
ſpreading Dome; and without them, a Cloyſter almoſt encircling it.   Over each of the Entrances is
a Dome of ſmaller Dimenſion, curiouſly wrought
with variety of *Moſaic*.   The Eighth Gate-way is
                                        appropriated

appropriated to the Stair-Cafe, the Well of which is Oval; the Steps, which are of Stone, eafy of Afcent; adhering to the Wall at one End, but feem rather to be upheld by the Iron Rail that is upon them, than fupported underneath at the other: This is deemed a curious Piece of Mafonry; but is not the only one of the Kind in *Oxford.* The Awe we are ftruck with at entering into the Grand *Area* of the Library, we leave to the Experience of thofe who feel it; as it is not eafily defcribed. The Pavement is of different coloured Stone, brought from *Harts-Foreft* in *Germany.* The Piers or Butments of the Arches are adorned with Pilafters of the *Ionic* Order.

The Dome, which is 46 Feet high from the Pavement, is wrought in curious Compartments in Stucco. It is chiefly lighted by Windows in the Cylindric Part thereof; between which, are Treffes of Fruits and Flowers. In the circular Part, without the Piers, are the Book-Cafes and Reading-Tables; this Part is lighted by the fmall fquare Windows; which are thus proportioned and difpofed, to admit of a Gallery above, which would otherwife have been too high; this Gallery is appropriated to the fame Ufes as the circular Part beneath. Over the Door is a very good Statue of the Founder by *Rysbrac:* The beft Point to view it from, is, directly oppofite to it, in the Gallery. The firft Stone of this fuperb Building was laid *May* 17, A. D. 1737; and being compleatly finifhed, was opened on *Thurfday, April* 13, 1749; when the Duke of *Beaufort,* at the Requeft of the other Truftees, *viz.* the Earl of *Oxford,* Sir *Walter Wagftaff Bagot,* and Sir *Watkin Williams Wynne,* Baronets, and *Edward Smith,* Efq; performed the Ceremony, by making a fhort, but elegant Speech

in

in *Latin*, and delivering the Keys into the Hands of the Rev. Dr. *John Purnel* then Vice-Chancellor; who, in the Name of the Univerfity, returned Thanks to the Truftees for their faithful Difcharge of the Truft repofed in them, in a fhort *Latin* Speech likewife.

The Librarian is appointed by the Great Officers of State; and not by the Truftees, or the Univerfity.

After the public Buildings, a Defcription of the PHYSIC GARDEN properly follows.[17] It lies at the Eaft End of the City, on the River *Cherwell*, oppofite to *Magdalen* College. This was the Donation of the Right Honourable *Henry D' Anvers*, Earl of *Danby*; who purchafed the Ground (containing five Acres) of *Magdalen* College, furrounded it with a lofty Wall, and erected, next to the Street, a Parapet with Iron Palifades thereon, and a Pair of Iron-Gates. The Piers which fupport thefe and the other Iron-work, being properly ornamented, with *Vafes* of Fruits and Flowers of various Kinds; the whole ferving as a Fence to the Green-Court, through which we pafs to the Gate-way or Grand-Entrance.

This Gate-way is juftly efteemed an elegant Piece of Architecture. The Defign is afcribed to *Inigo Jones*; nor is it unworthy of fuch an Architect: The Manner of it is thus: It is of the *Doric* Proportion, but without Triglyphs. The Columns and other Parts of the Building are curioufly wrought with *Ruftic*. The Frontifpiece confifts of two fmall Pediments, and one of larger Dimenfion; which, at its Extremities, partly covers the other two, and the whole mantled over with Lead ; fo that neither Snow or Rain can lodge to damage the Fabric. In
the

the Center over the Arch is a Buft of the Founder, Lord *Danby*.   On the Left-hand of the Entrance is a Statue of CHARLES I. and on the Right-hand, one of CHARLES II.   The Niches thefe ftand in are finifhed by the two fmall Pediments above-mentioned.   On the Face of the *Corona* and the *Frize* is the following Infcription; viz. *Gloriæ Dei optimi maximi Honori* Caroli I. *Regis in Ufum Academiæ & Reipublicæ* Henricus *Comes* Danby, Anno 1632.   This Infcription is likewife on the Garden Front.

The Garden is divided into four Quarters, with a broad Walk down the Middle, a crofs Walk, and one all round.   Near the Entrance, one on the Right, the other on the Left, are two elegant and ufeful *Green-houfes*, built by the Univerfity for *Exotics* ; of which there are as confiderable a Col-lection, as can be met with any where.   One of the large Aloes was blown in 1750, and grew to the Height of 21 Feet.[18]   In the Quarters, within the Yew Hedges, are the greateft Variety imaginable of fuch Plants, that require no artificial Heat to nourifh them, all ranged in their proper Claffes, and numbered.

At the lower End of the middle Walk, near the Iron Gates, are two magnificent Yew-Trees, cut in the Form of Pedeftals, (but of enormous Size) with a Flower-Pot on the Top, and a Plant, as it were, growing out of it; the whole (of each) being one fingle Tree only.

Eaftward of the Garden, without the Walls, is an excellent Hot-Houfe ; where tender Plants, fuch whofe native Soil lies between the Tropics, are raif-ed and brought to great Perfection ; viz. the Anana or Pine-Apple, the Plantain, the Coffee Shrub, the Caper Tree, the Cinnamon, the Creeping Cereus,

and

and many others.   Thefe Pine-Apples have nearly
the fame delicious Flavour as thofe raifed in warm-
er Climates; the Caper and the Coffee Shrub alfo
bear well.

The Earl fettled an annual Revenue for the Maintenance of the Garden, and furnifhed it with Plants
and Herbs, for the Ufe of fuch Gentlemen of the
Univerfity who ftudy Botany, as a neceffary Branch
of Phyfic.

This ufeful Foundation has been much improved
by the late Dr. *Sherard*, who brought from *Smyrna*
a valuable Collection of Plants.   He built a Library, adjoining to the Garden, for Botanical Books,
and furnifhed it with a curious Collection.   One
End of this Building hath, within a few Years,
been altered into a convenient Apartment for the
Profeffor, whofe Salary is paid out of the Intereft
of 3000 *l*. given by Dr. *Sherard* for that Purpofe.
The Affiftant to the Profeffor is paid by the Univerfity.

Having given our Reader a fhort Account of
the Rife and Progrefs of the Univerfity, a Defcription of the City and its Situation, and likewife of the Public Buildings, &c: Proceed we in
the next Place, to defcribe and give fome Account
of the feveral Colleges; and as *Magdalen* College
is the neareft to the Place we laft mentioned, and
the firft we meet with in the Road from *London*, it
may not be improper to begin with that.[19]

MAGDALEN

MAGDALEN COLLEGE.

THE College of St. *Mary Magdalen* is situated without the Eaſt-gate, upon the River *Cherwell:* We enter it by a handſome Portal in the *Doric* Order, having in a Niche a Statue of the Founder. The firſt Thing worthy the Attention of a curious Obſerver, is the Weſt Entrance into the *Chapel*; over which are five ſmall hiſtorical Figures, of elegant Sculpture. That on the Right, in a kneeling Poſture, repreſents the *Founder*; the next,*William* of *Wickham* the Founder of the two St. *Mary Winton* Colleges,where he was educated; that in the Middle, S. *Mary Magdalen*, to whom the College is dedicated; the next, in a kneeling Poſture, King *Henry* III. who founded the Hoſpital which was converted into this College; and that on the Left, St. *John the Baptiſt*, to whom the ſaid Hoſpital was dedicated.

The Building on the Left-Hand is the Preſident's Lodgings; adjoining to which is a magnificent Gothic Gate-way (formerly the Grand-Entrance into the College) with an Obſervatory over it, adorned with Statues as big as the Life, of four of the above Perſons, viz. the *Founder*, St. *Mary Magdalen*, King *Henry* III. and St. *John the Baptiſt*.

One Particular in this and the Chapel Gateway which demands our Notice, is a ſmall ſlender Arch, ſeparate and diſtinct from the other curve Mouldings; this, no doubt, was formerly eſteemed curious Maſonry.

Between the Chapel and the above Gateway we enter the Cloyſter; near this Entrance is the com-

mon

mon Way from moſt Parts of the College into the
Chapel; which is a well-proportioned Edifice in
form of a *Roman* T inverted. The Anti Chapel
is remarkable for two beautiful Staff-moulded Pillars, and ſome elegant Monuments; particularly
one, on the Left-Hand of the Organ-Loft, erected
to the Memory of two Brothers of the Name of
Lyttleton, who were drowned in the River *Cherwell*; one by endeavouring to ſave the other.

The Weſt Window, painted in *Claro Obſcuro*,
was done after a Deſign of *Schwart*'s which he
made and executed for the Wife of *William* Duke
of *Bavaria*, upwards of 200 Years ago; as appears
by a Print lately purchaſed by the Society, engraved
by *Sadeler* from the Original. It repreſents the
Reſurrection; and, by the above Print, was cer-
tainly a grand Deſign: But at preſent the Beauty
of it is much impaired. In the Time of the Civil
Wars, all the Windows, being painted in the
ſame Manner, were taken down and ſecreted in
different Places; but it unfortunately happened,
that thoſe belonging to the inner Chapel, after diligent Search, were diſcovered by a Party of *Cromwell*'s Soldiers; and by them brought into the
Cloyſter, ſpread upon the Pavement, and trampled
on, till they were entirely demoliſhed.[20] Thoſe
now in the Chapel were removed thither from the
Anti-Chapel in 1741; but not being a ſufficient
Number to completely glaze the whole, two New-
ones have ſince been added.

The Altar-Piece was painted by *Iſaac Fuller*,
an *Engliſh* Hiſtory Painter who flouriſhed about 90
Years ago; who having ſtudied and admired the
muſcular Manner of *Michael Angelo*, ſeems to have
neglected the graceful Elegance of *Raphael*: For
although many of the Figures may juſtly be deemed

ed excellent Anatomical or Academy Drawings; yet for want of that eaſy and natural Diſpoſition, peculiar to the laſt-mention'd great Maſter, and better Colouring, the whole appears crude and unpleaſing. This Painting, however, gave occaſion to the Writing of an excellent *Latin* Poem by Mr. *Addiſon*; (ſometime Fellow of this College) which may be ſeen in the *Muſæ Anglicanæ*.

Underneath this Piece of the Reſurrection by *Fuller*, is an admirable Picture of our Saviour bearing his Croſs, ſuppoſed to be painted by *Guido*. It was taken at *Vigo*, and brought into *England* by the late Duke of *Ormond*: But afterwards falling into the Hands of *William Freman*, Eſq; of *Hamels* in *Hertfordſhire*, he gave it to the College. To this worthy Gentleman the College is likewiſe chiefly obliged for an excellent Organ, two additional Bells to the Peal of Eight, and another very conſiderable Benefaction. We ſhould not do Juſtice to the Memory of this true Friend to the Univerſity, unleſs we mentioned an Inſtance or two more of his Affection for it. Many Years ſucceſſively, before we were ſo unfortunate to loſe him, he conſtantly ſpent a Month or two in the Summer here; during which Time, he reſided in College, and conformed to an academical Life. By his laſt Will he bequeathed the Reverſion of an Eſtate to the College, and an Organ, which then ſtood at *Hamels*, to the *Muſic-Room* in *Oxford*, provided there ſhould be no Inſtrument of that Kind in it, at the Time of his Death; otherwiſe to be erected in the Hall belonging to this College: But the former happening to be the Caſe, it accordingly went thither; for which the Public in

general,

general, as well as the Musical Society in particular, are obliged to him.[21]

But to return: The Altar has been built, in
the present Manner, a few Years only; the Design is elegant, and the Workmanship well performed: Besides the common Embellishments of
the Corinthian Order, there are Festoons over
every Pannel (extremely well carved) which
greatly enrich it. The Wainscotting on each
Side is intended to be carried on to the Screen.

Each Window contains six Figures, nearly
as big as the Life, representing the Apostles, primitive Fathers, Saints and Martyrs. Most People think this Room rather too dark at first entering it, but afterwards are better reconciled:
The occasion of that Opinion is, undoubtedly,
the Contrast between this and the Anti-Chapel;
which they pass through to it, and is extremely
light. Cathedral Service is performed here e-
very Day at Eleven and Four, except *Sundays*
and Holidays, and then the Morning Prayers
begin at Eight, on Account of the University
Sermon.

From hence, on the Right, we pass into the
Cloyster which encompasses the great Quadrangle, and remains in its primitive State: The
whole making the most venerable Appearance of
any College in *Oxford*, having undergone the
fewest Alterations of any since it was founded.
On the South Side are the Hall and Chapel; on
the West the President's old Lodgings and the
Library; and on the North and East, the Lodgings of the Fellows, Demies, &c.[22] At the South-
East Corner of the Cloyster, is the Way up to
the Hall; which is a very spacious Room, handsomely fitted up, and adorned with four whole
length

length Pourtraits, viz. of the *Founder*, Dr. *Butler*
the late Prefident, *William Freman*, Efq; in his Dr.
of Laws Robe, and *Prince Rupert*; two Half-
lengths, viz. Bifhop *Warner*, a great Benefactor to
the *Library*, and Dr *Hammond.*

The interior Part of this Quadrangle is ornamented with Hieroglyphics, of which, (though a celebrated Antiquary * hath been pleafed to call them
*whimfical Figures, which ferve to amufe the Vulgar,
but are only the licentious Inventions of the Mafon,*)
we fhall here give a particular, and, we truft, a ra-
tional Account, from a Latin † Manufcript in the
Library of this College.

Beginning, therefore, from the South-Weft
Corner, the two firft Figures we meet with are the
Lion, and the *Pelican.* The former of thefe is the
Emblem of *Courage* and *Vigilance,* the latter of
parental Tendernefs, and Affection. Both of them
together exprefs to us the complete Character of a
good Governor of a College. Accordingly they are
placed under the Windows of thofe Lodgings,
which, originally, belonged to the Prefident, as
the Inftructions they convey ought particularly to
regulate his Conduct.

Going on to the right Hand, on the other fide
of the Gate-way, are four Figures, viz. the *School-
mafter,* the *Laywer,* the *Phyfician,* and the *Divine.*

* See Dr. *Stukeley*'s Itinerarium Curiofum. p. 42.
† This Piece is intituled *Oedipus Magdalenenfis: Explicatio v'z:
Imaginum, & Figurarum, quæ apud Magdalenenf-s in interiori Collegii
Quadrangulo Tibicinibus impofitæ vifuntur.* It was written by Mr.
William Reeks, fometime Fellow of this College, at the Requeft of
Dr. *Clerk,* who was Prefident from the year 1671, to 1687, and to
whom it is infcribed. It is divided into two Parts. In the firft,
the general Doctrine of Hieroglyphics is very learnedly difcuffed.
In the latter, he defcends to a particular Confideration of the
Hieroglyphics at *Magdalene*; and from this Part the Account here
given is extracted.

Thefe

These are ranged along the outside of the Library, and represent the Duties and Business of the Students of the House. By means of Learning in general, they are to be introduced to one of the three learned Professions, or else, as is hinted to us by the Figure with *Cap and Bells* in the Corner, they must turn out *Fools* in the End.

We come now to the North Side of the Quadrangle, and here the first three Figures represent the History of *David*, his Conquest over the *Lion* and *Goliah*; from whence we are taught, not to be discouraged at any Difficulties that may stand in our way, as the *Vigour of Youth* will easily enable us to surmount them. The next Figure to these is that of the *Hippopotamos*, or *River-Horse*, carrying his young one upon his Shoulders. This is the Emblem of a good Tutor, or Fellow of a College, who is set to watch over the Youth of the Society, and by whose Prudence they are to be led through the Dangers of their first Entrance into the World. The Figure immediately following represents *Sobriety*, or *Temperance*, that most necessary Virtue of a Collegiate Life. The whole remaining Train of Figures are the Vices we are instructed to avoid. Those next to Temperance are the opposite Vices of *Gluttony*, and *Drunkenness*. Then follow the *Lucanthropos*, the *Hyæna*, and *Panther*, representing *Violence*, *Fraud*, and *Treachery*; the *Gryphin* representing *Covetousness*, and the next Figure *Anger*, or *Moroseness*. The *Dog*, the *Dragon*, the *Deer*, *Flattery*, *Envy*, and *Timidity*; and the three last, the *Mantichora*, the *Boxers*, and the *Lamia*, *Pride*, *Contention*, and *Lust*.

We have here, therefore, a complete and instructive Lesson, for the use of a Society dedicated to the Advancement of Religion and Learning;
and,

and, on this Plan, we may suppose the Founder of *Magdalen* thus speaking, by means of these Figures, to the Students of his College.

" It is your Duty, who live under the Care of a President, whose *Vigilance,* and *parental Tenderness,* are the proper Qualifications to support the Government of my House, attentively to pursue your Studies, in your *several Professions* ; and so to avoid the *Follies* of an idle, unlettered, and dissipated Course of Life. You may possibly meet with many *Difficulties,* at your first setting out in this Road, but these every *Stripling* will be able to overcome by *Courage and Perseverance.* And remember, when you are advanced beyond these Difficulties, that it is your Duty to lend your Assistance to those who come after you, and whose Education is committed to your Care. You are to be an Example to them of *Sobriety,* and *Temperance :* So shall you guard them from falling into the Snares of *Excess,* and *Debauchery.* You shall teach them that the Vices with which the World abounds, *Cruelty, Fraud, Avarice, Anger* and *Envy,* as well as the more supple ones of abject *Flattery,* and *Cowardice,* are not to be countenanced within these hallowed Retirements. And let it be your Endeavour to avoid *Pride* and *Contention,* the Parents of Faction, and in your Situation, the worst and most unnatural of all Factions, the *Faction of the Cloyster.* And lastly, you will complete the *Collegiate Character,* if you crown all your other Acquirements with the unspotted *Purity,* and *Chastity,* of your Lives and Conversation."

We hope, by this Time, the Reader is convinced, that so exact a System of Morals, could

not

not eafily have been produced from the *licentious Inventions of the Mafon.*

From the Cloyfter we go through a narrow Paffage in the North-Side, into the Court where the new Building ftands. This Edifice is 300 Feet in Length, and confifts of three Stories above the Cellars, befide the Garrets. This Front is fupported by an *Arcade,* which forms a beautiful Cloyfter. The whole is built of *Heddington* Stone, and is juftly deemed an elegant Structure. It has confiderably the Advantage of fome other modern Buildings: For whereas the *upper Story* of thofe is commonly an *Attic,* and confequently the Rooms lower than thofe of the *middle Story;* the Rooms in the upper Story here are exactly of the fame Dimenfion with thofe below; and command a better Profpect. Three other Sides were originally intended to be added; but probably fince the Effect of that beautiful Opening to the Meadow has been feen, * the Society may think proper, in fome Refpect, to alter their Defign.

One unparalleled Beauty belonging to this College is the extenfive Out-let. The Grove feems perfectly adapted to indulge Contemplation; being a pleafant Kind of Solitude, laid out in Walks, and well planted with Elms and other large Trees. It has likewife a Bowling-Green in it, and having fome beautiful Lawns, feeds about forty Head of Deer.

Befide the Walks which are in the Grove there is a very delightful, and much frequented One, round a Meadow containing about 13 Acres, and that furrounded by the feveral Branches of

* See the Perfpective View annexed.

the

MAGDALEN COLL. NEW BUILDING

the *Cherwell*; from whence it is called the *Water-walk*.

This Walk yields all the Variety that could be wished for: Some Parts of it running in straight Lines, with the Trees regularly cut; others winding, and the Trees growing little otherwise than as Nature directs: There is plenty of Water as well as Verdure, and an agreeable View of the Country adjacent.

This College was founded by *William Patten*, usually called *William* of *Wainfleet*, from a Village of that Name in *Lincolnshire*, where he was born, and where there is a School which is kept in Repair by the College. He was first educated at *Winchester* School, and was afterwards Fellow of *New* College in *Oxford*. Having taken the Degree of Bachelor of Divinity, he was appointed chief Master of *Winchester* School, where he continued 12 Years, and then was made Provost of *Eaton* College by King *Henry* VI. who preferred him to the Bishopric of *Winchester* in the Year 1447, and in 1449 he was constituted Lord High Chancellor of *England*.

He first founded a Hall in *Oxford* without the East-Gate, which he dedicated to the Honour of St. *Mary Magdalen*, and in the Year 1456 obtained Leave of King *Henry* VI. to convert St. *John*'s Hospital, situated further Eastward, into a College, which the Hospitallers thereupon surrendered to Trustees for that Use, with all their Manors, Lands, and Possessions; in Consideration whereof there were settled on the said Hospitallers certain Pensions during their Lives; and the same Year the Bishop being impower'd by a Royal Charter to found his College on the Scite of the Hospital, he erected the great Quadrangle

with

with the Cloyſter about it, the Chambers and
Library, the Chapel and Hall alſo in his Life-
time; he likewiſe dedicated his College to St.
Mary Magdalen; and ordained that it ſhould for
ever bear her Name, notwithſtanding he further
devoted it in honour of all the tutelar Saints of
the Cathedral Church of *Wincheſter*, viz. the
bleſſed Virgin *Mary*, St. *John the Baptiſt*, St.
Peter, St. *Paul*, and the glorious Confeſſor St.
Swithin. And having choſen Fellows, &c. from
the Hall adjoining and other Seminaries, he further ordained, that this Foundation ſhould be a
perpetual College for poor and indigent Clerks
in the Univerſity of *Oxford*, ſtudying Arts and
Sciences. It conſiſts of a *Preſident*, forty *Fellows*, thirty Demies, a Divinity Lecturer, a School
Maſter and Uſher, four Chaplains, an Organiſt,
eight Clerks, and ſixteen Choriſters. The whole
Number of Students in their Books 108. King
Henry VI. likewiſe gave to the Founder the Hoſpital of St. *James* at *Brackley* in *Northamptonſhire* ;
which he annexed to the College as a Place for
the Society to retire to, in caſe a peſtilential Diſ-
temper or any other Cauſe ſhould render their
Reſidence here unſafe.

　Among the ſubſequent Benefactors to this College was *William Fitz-Alan*, Earl of *Arundel*,
who ſtipulated with the Preſident and Fellows,
(1 *Rich*. III.) that they and their Succeſſors for
ever ſhould celebrate daily Maſs for the Soul of
himſelf, the Soul of his Son *Thomas Maltravers*,
and the Souls of his Anceſtors, at an Altar from
thence called the *Arundel Altar*; and that all
Doctors and Maſters of this College ſhould mention Them, as well in their Prayers at *Oxford*,
as before their Sermons at St. *Paul*'s in *London*;
　　　　　　　　　　　　　　　　　　but

but the Maſſes have been diſuſed ever ſince the Reformation; in lieu of which there are annual Commemorations for the Benefactors, and quarterly Ones for the Founder. A Prayer likewiſe including both is daily read.

It is cuſtomary on St. *John Baptiſt*'s Day to have the Univerſity Sermon preached in the Stone Pulpit at the South-Eaſt Corner of the firſt Court within the College Gate; the Court on that Occaſion being decked with Boughs and ſtrewed with Ruſhes: Alluding to St. *John*'s preaching in the Wilderneſs, and in Commemoration of the Hoſpital's being dedicated to him. But if the Weather proves unfavourable, they adjourn into the Chapel; becauſe there is no Covering to ſhelter the Vice-Chancellor, &c. from the Inclemency of it; or any Accommodation as to ſitting except Benches placed on the Ground.

All this Side of the Building, except the Tower, are the Remains of the ſaid Hoſpital. Near one Half of which, viz. from the Weſt End running towards the Bridge, was the Chapel thereof 'till ſince the Reſtoration: But during the Civil Wars, and afterwards, having been profaned and proſtituted to the vileſt Purpoſes, the College obtained Leave to convert it into Lodgings. At the Weſt End in a ſmall Niche is the Head of the Baptiſt.

The laſt Thing we ſhall take Notice of, is the Tower. This was erected by the College under the Direction of Cardinal *Wolſey*, who was Fellow and (at that Time) Burſar of this College. It is about 150 Feet high, and by its ſolid and ſubſtantial Baſis, number of Set-offs, and gradual Diminution, is calculated for Strength and Duration as much as any Building whatever;

I   ever;

ever; it is nevertheleſs beautiful, and a great Ornament to the Place.

The moſt advantageous View of it, is from the Phyſic Garden. We muſt not omit mentioning that this Tower contains a very muſical Peal of Ten Bells; and that on *May* Day Morning the Clerks and Choriſters aſſemble on the Top of it, and inſtead of a Maſs of Requiem for King *Henry* VII. ſing chearful Songs and Catches.[23]

Their Viſitor is the Biſhop of *Wincheſter.*[24]

Late and preſent Preſidents,[25]

1722. Dr. *Edward Butler*, LL. D. a Member of Parliament for the Univerſity.

1745. Dr. *Jenner*, *Margaret* Profeſſor of Divinity.

❁❁❁❁❁❁❁❁❁❁❁❁❁❁❁❁

QUEEN's COLLEGE.

THE next College, after we have paſſed St. *Mary Magdalen*, is *Queen*'s, which ſtands within the Eaſt-Gate, on the North Side of the *High-ſtreet.*

The whole Area, on which this fine College is built, is an oblong Square, of 300 Feet in Length, and 220 in Breadth, which being divided by the Hall and Chapel, forms two ſpacious Courts.

The South End, which is the grand Front, abuts upon the *High-ſtreet*, in the Middle whereof is a magnificent Gate, and over it the Statue of Queen *Caroline*, under a Cupola ſupported by Pillars; the reſt of the Front being adorned with Niches, but no Chambers on this Side, except at each End.

The

The firſt, or South Court, is a handſome Quadrangle, 140 Feet long, and 130 broad, having
a lofty Cloiſter, ſupported by ſquare Pillars, on
the Weſt and South, and another Cloiſter deſigned on the Eaſt. Over the Weſt Cloiſter are
two Stories, conſiſting of the Chambers of the
Fellows and Students, an elegant Gallery and
common Room ; and in that Cloiſter is the A-
partment of the Provoſt. Over the Eaſt Cloiſter alſo are deſigned Chambers for the Fellows
and Students, to be built exactly like thoſe already erected. The ſecond, or North Court,
is 130 Feet long, and 90 broad, having the Library over it on the Weſt, and Chambers for the
Fellows and Students on the North, Eaſt, and
South.

The Buildings are in general very fine, but
thoſe that are moſt admired are the Chapel, the
Hall and the Library.

The Chapel is 100 Feet long, and 30 broad.
In the arched Roof is a Piece of Painting by Sir
James Thornhill. The Windows are admirably
painted ; the Subject of that over the Altar, by
Mr. *Price* in 1717, is the Nativity of our Saviour. The Side Windows were remov'd thither
from the old Chapel ; two on the North Side are
the laſt Judgment, and two others on the South,
the Aſcenſion. The reſt are all of old Glaſs,
remarkable for the Livelineſs of the Colours.

There is a Paſſage between the Chapel and
the Hall from the South to the North Court, the
Walls of which carry a handſome Cupola with
eight Ionic Columns, and all the proper Ornaments of that Order. The Outſide of the whole
is a Doric Building, and the Inſide of the Hall
beautified with the ſame Order : But the Inſide

E of

of the Chapel is entirely Corinthian, the Ceiling
of which being Fretwork is not inferior to that
Order.

The Hall is 60 Feet long, and 30 broad, with
an arched Roof of a suitable Height, and appears
to be one of the best-proportioned Rooms in
Oxford. It is extremely well illuminated, and
has a Chimney-Piece of beautiful Marble; and
there is an Opening from the Gallery over the
West Cloister, which seems designed for Music;
and hither Strangers are frequently brought, who
desire to see the Society at Dinner.

The Library on the West Side of the North
Court about 123 Feet in length, and 55 in height,
is a noble Building of the Corinthian Order, with
a spacious Cloister to the East, and the Statue
of the Founder, and principal Benefactors to the
College in Niches to the West. 'Tis adorned
with beautiful Classes, and furnished with a curious and valuable Collection of Books and Manuscripts in most Languages and Sciences.

Robert Egglesfield, a Native of *Cumberland*, Con-
fessor to Queen *Philippa*, and Batchelor of Divinity in this University, having purchased several
Tenements in the Parish of St. *Peter*'s in the *East*,
erected there a Collegiate Hall, at the Instance
(and, probably by the Encouragement) of Queen
Philippa, Consort of King *Edward* III. giving it
the Name of *Aula Scholarium Reginæ de* Oxon;
and on the 18th of *January* 1340, obtained the
Royal Charter for incorporating the Society of
this Hall or College; by virtue whereof he constituted a Provost and twelve Fellows, ordering,
that the Provost should be chosen out of the Fellows, and be in Holy Orders; and that for the
future

future the Fellows should be elected out of the
Counties of *Cumberland* and *Westmorland*.

The principal Benefactors, besides the Founder, were King *Edward* III. and his Queen *Philippa*; King *Charles* I. who gave this College three
Rectories and three Vicarages in *Hampshire*; Sir
Joseph Williamson, Knight, sometime Fellow,
who rebuilt part of the College, and left 6000 *l.*
towards the finishing of it, besides a most valuable Library of Books; Dr. *Barlow*, Bishop of
Lincoln, also gave his Books to this Library;
Dr. *Lancaster*, the Provost of this College, and
Dr. *Timothy Halton*, were great Benefactors. And
of late several very considerable Exhibitions have
been given by Sir *Francis Bridgman*, Lady *Elizabeth Hastings*, and Mr. *Michel* of *Richmond*.

The Chamber over the old Gate, opposite St.
Edmund's Hall, was the Habitation of King
Henry V. when he studied in this College.

The East Window of the old Chapel, which
is still standing, is reckon'd a curious Piece of
Gothic Architecture.

The Members in this College are one Provost,
sixteen Fellows, two Chaplains, eight Taberdars
(so called from Taberdum, a short Gown which
they formerly wore) 16 Scholars, two Clerks, and
forty Exhibitioners; besides a great Number of
Masters, Batchelors, Gentlemen Commoners,
Commoners, and other Students.

A Custom here is, that they are call'd to Dinner and Supper by Sound of the Trumpet, and
when the Fellows, as the Founder's Statutes direct, have placed themselves on the further
Side of the Table, the Taberdars kneel before
them on the opposite Side of the Table, and on
Sundays and Holidays dispute on some of the most

E 2   controverted

controverted Queſtions in Divinity; and on other
Days render ſome Parts of *Ariſtotle*'s Rhetorick,
Poeticks, or Ethicks.

Another Cuſtom is, that the Burſar of the
College on *New-Year*'s Day gives each Member
a Needle and Thread, ſaying, *Take this, and be
thrifty*, as a Rebus on the Founder's Name
(*Aiguille*) in *French*, ſignifying a Needle, and
Fil, a Thread, *Egglesfield*.

Another is, having a Boar's Head on *Chriſt-
mas* Day, uſher'd in very ſolemnly with a celebrated Monkiſh Song, in Memory of a *Taberdar*'s
killing a wild Boar in *Shotover* Wood.

The Viſitor is the Archbiſhop of *York*.

The preſent Provoſt.

1730. *Joſeph Smith*, D. D.

❀ ❀

New COLLEGE.

NEW College is ſituated North of *Queen*'s,
from which it is ſeparated only by a narrow
Lane.

We enter this College by a magnificent Portal or Gateway, leading into the firſt Court,
which is a Quadrangle of about 168 Feet long,
and about 129 broad, with a Statue of *Minerva*
in the Middle of it, the Donation of *Henry Parker*, Eſq; ſometime Fellow of this College. This
Court as built at the Foundation of the College,
was low and with narrow arch'd tranſom Windows, in the Faſhion of the Times: But ſoon
after the Reſtoration of King *Charles* II. another
Story was added over the old Building, and all
the Windows altered to their preſent Form
with

with Sashes. On the North Side is the Chapel and the Hall; on the East the Library; on the South the Fellows Apartments, and on the West the Warden's Lodgings, which are large and commodious, well finished and beautifully furnished, among others, with some scarce and valuable Portraits.

In the North-West Corner of this Court is the Entrance into the Chapel; by much the grandest in the University. The Form of it is like that at *Magdalen* College, but larger. The Anti-Chapel is supported (like that) by two beautiful Staff-moulded Pillars; but of greater Magnitude. This Part is upwards of 80 Feet long, and 36 broad: The inner Chapel 100 Feet long, 35 broad, and 65 high. As we enter the Chantry or inner Chapel the most striking Object is the Altar-piece; the Painting whereof was done by our ingenious Countryman Mr. *Henry Cook*, who flourished near sixty Years ago. It represents the Concave of a *Semi-Rotunda* in the Ionic Order, with a Cupola adorned with curious Mosaic Work; in which, the East-End of the Chapel seems to terminate. The Altar which is partly built of Wood and partly painted, intercepting in some Degree the View at right Angles, greatly favours the *Deceptio*; particularly, two large open Pannels in the lower Part thereof, which have a wonderful Effect.

In the upper Part of the Altar, which is painted in such a Manner as to seem the Finishing of the Wood-work that supports it, between two Columns of the Composite Order rising in just Proportion to the Corinthian below, is a Frame and Pannel, wherein is represented the Salutation of the Virgin *Mary:* And above the Entablature hangs hovering a most beautiful Cloud with great

E 3   Numbers

Numbers of Angels and Cherubs in various Attitudes, waiting the return of the Angel *Gabriel*. The proper Place to view it from to Advantage, is the Entrance into the Choir; the Perspective being contrived on purpose, to answer that Height and Distance. The Communion Table and the center Pannel are covered with Crimson Velvet, and the whole is enclosed within a Rail of curious wrought Iron-work; the Former the Gift of Dr. *Burton* the present Master of *Winchester* School, the latter of Mr. *Terry*, late Fellow.

Next to this the Windows on the South Side are most attracting to the Eyes of Strangers: Each Window containing eight Portraits as big as the Life, of Saints and Martyrs, done by Mr. *Price* of *London*. These the late worthy Warden with the Concurrence of the Society began in 1737, at the Expence of 100 *l. per* Window, which was defrayed out of a certain Fund set a-part for repairing and beautifying the College; but not to exhaust it too hastily, only one Window a Year was completed: However this Work was assisted by some Legacies and Benefactions. The Stalls are remarkably elegant in the Gothic Manner: But the painted Figures in the Pannels somewhat Disgrace the Architecture.

The *Brass* Sconces against the Stalls and on the Desks, together with two large and beautiful Branches suspended at the Ends of two long gilded Chains in the Middle of the Choir, are very great Embellishments: The latter were the Gift of Dr. *Cheyney*, the present Dean of *Winchester*.

Here is a most excellent Organ first built by —— *Dclham*; and since improved by Mr. *John Byfield*, who added the Clarion Stop, and the Swelling Organ. Cathedral Service is performed

formed here twice a Day, viz. at Eleven and Five; except *Sundays* and Holidays, and then the Morning Prayers begin at Eight as at *Magdalen* College. This Room is efteemed one of the beft in *England* for Mufic: which probably is owing to its being very fpacious, and having no Breaks (fuch as Arches and Side-Ifles) to divide the Sounds. Upon the whole; when the Windows on the North-Side are perfected in the fame Manner with thofe on the South, which they are intended fhortly to be, this Room will furpafs almoft every Thing of the Kind.

Adjoining to the Chapel is a fpacious Cloifter which forms a Quadrangle 146 Feet one Way, and 105 the other; on the North Side of which is a lofty Tower containing a pleafant Peal of Ten Bells.

The Way up to the Hall is at the North-Eaft Corner of the Quadrangle; it is 78 Feet long, 35 broad, and 43 high. It is handfomely wainfcotted and floor'd, and adorned with the Portraits of the Founder *William* of *Wickam*, *William* of *Wainfleet* the Founder of *Magdalen* College, and Archbifhop *Chicheley* the Founder of *All-Souls*, both Fellows of this College in the Founder's Life-time.

The Library (fituate on the Eaft Side of the Quadrangle) confifts of two Rooms, one over the other, 70 Feet long and 22 broad; both of them well furnifhed with Books, particularly fome hundreds of valuable Manufcripts.

From hence we pafs through the middle Gate into the Garden-Court, which widens by Breaks as we approach the Garden-Gate. This Court is feparated from the Garden, by an Iron Gate and Palifade which extend 130 Feet in Length, and admit of a moft agreeable Profpect of the Garden through them. In the middle of the Garden is a beautiful Mount with an eafy Afcent to the Top of it, and the Walks round about it, as well as the Summit of it, guarded with Yew Hedges. The Area before the Mount being divided into four Quarters, in one is the King's Arms, with the Garter and Motto; in that oppofite to it the Founder's; in the Third a Sun Dial, and the Fourth a Garden-Knot; all planted in Box and neatly cut.

The whole is furrounded by a Terras. On each Side are Lime-Trees planted; and on the North Side in particular there is a *ferpentine Walk* planted with *flowring Shrubs*. Behind the Mount likewife is a fine Collection of Shrubs fo contrived as to rife gradually one above the other, and over them, a Row of Horfe Chefnut Trees, which fpread in fuch a Manner as to cover the Garden Wall, and carry the Eye on to a moft beautiful Mantle of tall Elms, which terminates the View, and feems to be the only Boundary to that End of the Garden; but we are obliged to *Magdalen* College Grove for this additional Beauty.

At the South Eaft Corner of the Garden we enter the BOWLING-GREEN; which is in all Refpects neat and commodious. Oppofite to the Entrance is a *Pavilion* or *Temple*; on the Right a Terras with flowring Shrubs, and a Row of Elms to fhade the Green in the Evening, that Side being almoft due Weft; and on the Left a Row of Sycomores which are mentioned by Dr. *Plot*, in his *Natural Hiftory* of *Oxfordfhire*, as a great Curiofity; being incorporated from one End of the Row to the other.

Having conducted our Reader to the furtheft Part of the College, he may return at his Leifure: But before he leaves the Garden, we would recommend

NEW COLLEGE FROM THE MOUNT.

mend to him a View of the Building from the Mount; whence the Garden-Court, in particular, has a very grand Effect: For from thence the Wings appear properly diſplay'd, and the whole is ſeen at a convenient Diſtance. The Perſpective View annexed was taken from the firſt Landing-place, and may be compared with the Original. From the Top of the Mount likewiſe there is an extenſive and agreeable Proſpect of the Country, and of ſome other Buildings in the Univerſity.

In the Muniment Houſe belonging to this College is preſerv'd the large ancient Croſier of the Founder, which is Silver gilt, almoſt entire, very maſſive and weighty, finely wrought and curiouſly embelliſhed with variety of Figures of Seraphs and the tutelar Saints of the Cathedral of *Wincheſter*, Elevations, Temple Portals and Perſpectives; and (having lately been cleanſed) is one of the beſt preſerved Pieces of Antiquity of the Kind in *England*.

In a ſmall Court belonging to the Warden's Lodgings, and adjoining to the Lane leading to *Queen's* College, is part of a very ancient Mulberry Tree; which before the ſevere Winter in 1739, was diametrically ſawn aſunder at both Ends, and after having lain at length on the Ground (being intended for Fuel) above a full Year, part of which was that very Winter, it was raiſed up on a Stone-pitch'd Area againſt a Wall; with no other View but to remove the Inconvenience of its lying in the Way: But it ſoon began to put forth luxuriant Branches, and it has now large Limbs and bears great Quantities of Fruit every Year.

The laſt Curioſity we ſhall mention, is a beautiful elliptic Arch which is turned over the above Lane, for the Convenience of the Warden to paſs into his Garden without coming out at the College

Gate.

Gate. The Lane it is thrown over does not turn at Right-Angles from that leading to the College, but runs obliquely ; which renders the Contrivance of it the more artful and uncommon. A curious Observer will, nevertheless, if he examines the Ribs of the Arch, discover that they form straight Lines from the Abutments on one Side to those on the other, notwithstanding the Whole in a Front-view, seems a-twist.

This College was founded by Dr. *William Long*, a Native of *Wickham* in *Hampshire*, from whence he obtained the Name of *William* of *Wickham*. He was advanced by King *Edward* the Third, and his Successor *Richard* the Second, to some of the largest and most considerable Preferments in the Church; as Archdeacon of *Lincoln*, Prepos. of *Wells*, Rector of St *Mary*'s in *Southampton*, together with twelve Prebends; and afterwards was Keeper of the Privy Seal, Bishop of *Winchester*, and Lord High Chancellor of *England*. He maintained seventy Students in several Halls in *Oxford* for seven Years whilst the College was building for their Reception ; having in the Year 1379 obtained a Charter for their Incorporation. The Foundation Stone was laid *March* 5th, in the said Year ; and it was finished on *April* 14, 1386. when the Warden and Fellows took Possession of it by entering it in a solemn Procession. In the Year following, the other, St. *Mary*'s College near *Winchester* was begun, and was finished and inhabited in the Year 1393, by a Warden, ten Fellows, three Chaplains, three Clerks, and sixteen Choristers; as also two Masters and seventy Boys, out of whom a certain Number were to be annually elected as a Supply to *New College*, first by two of the Founder's Kinsmen, and then by the Senior on Roll successively. Both
which

which Colleges this moſt pious and munificent Founder ſaw completed, making ample Proviſion for the Support of each, and giving them ſo regular and perfect a Body of Statutes, that many ſucceeding Founders have compiled from them. And having ſurvived many Years, he enlarged his Will with coſtly Legacies of Jewels, Plate, Money, and Books, to be diſtributed throughout the ſeveral Dioceſes he was preferred in, or had temporal Poſſeſſions, at his Deceaſe, to pray (according to the Times) for his Soul, amounting to the Value of upwards of 6000 *l.* Sterling; an immenſe Sum according to the Value of Money in thoſe Days. He died about the 5th of *Henry* IV. in the Year 1404. when he was near 80 Years of Age.

It was ſtipulated between the Univerſity and the Founder, that the Fellows of this College ſhould be admitted to all Degrees on the firſt Day of the Term, without any Grace of the Congregation of the Maſters, or undergoing any Examination for them in the public Schools, provided they were examined in the College according to the Form of the Univerſity, and had their Graces given them in like Manner by the Warden and thirteen ſenior Fellows of the College conven'd and aſſembled for that Purpoſe.

The Univerſity Sermon is preached here every *Lady Day* and *Trinity Sunday* in the Anti-chapel: On which Occaſion the Choir attend and perform an Anthem in the Organ-Loft.

Another Cuſtom is the peculiar Manner of calling the Fellows to Dinner and Supper; namely, by a Choriſter's going from the Chapel Door to the Garden Gate at Twelve and Six, crying, *à Manger tous Seigneurs,* i. e *To Dinner or Supper Gentlemen all.*

The

The Benefactions to this College have been very numerous; all of which stand upon Record as so many laudable, and lasting Memorials of Respect, Honour and Gratitude to the Founder; the Benefactors having been chiefly Members of this Society.

The College Manors and Estates (as well those settled by the Founder as those by the several Benefactors abovementioned) are visited annually (but at two different Seasons) by the Warden, a Senior Fellow, appointed by the Society for that Purpose, and the regular Steward with their proper Attendants, which they call *Spring* and *Autumn Progress*; besides a Third called the *Home Progress*, executed about *Easter*, by the Sub-Warden attended by the Society and Servants in waiting, for visiting the Lands and Houses within the University.

A certain Time is appointed by the Wardens, commonly about the beginning of *September*, for an Election of the Scholars at *Winchester* School to succeed Yearly to this College; when the Warden, two Senior Fellows (during that Expedition called *Posers*) nominated by the select Governors of this College, called the *Thirteen*, for that Purpose, who together with the Warden, Sub-Warden, and Schoolmaster of *Winchester* meet and open their Election there, for examining, chusing and filling up Vacancies in the School, and to supply this Society within the Year, in manner as abovementioned. As also for redressing and regulating any Grievances and Inconveniencies in that College: Although the Warden and Fellows of *Winchester* are the immediate Governors and Inspectors of the School; and are nobly accommodated by the plentiful Provision made by that Part of the Founder's Bounty.

The

The prefent Members of this Society are one Warden, feventy Fellows, ten Chaplains, three Clerks, one Sexton, and fixteen Chorifters; the whole Number of Students of all Kinds being ufually about 115.

The Vifitor is the Bifhop of *Winchefter.*

Late and prefent Wardens.

1729 *John Coxed,* LL. D.

1740 *John Purnell,* D. D. Vice-Chancellor, from *Michaelmas* 1747 to *Michaelmas* 1750.

✻✻✻✻✻✻✻✻✻✻✻✻✻✻✻✻✻✻✻✻✻✻✻✻✻

UNIVERSITY COLLEGE.

U Niverfity College is fituated on the South Side of the *High-Street,* oppofite to that of *All-Souls,* the Front extending 260 Feet and upwards along the Street. This College confifts of two Courts, each of them having a handfome Gate, with a Tower over it, next the Street. The Weft Court, called the Old Court, is a regular Quadrangle of 100 Feet on every Side; the Eaft, or New Court, alfo is a regular Square, 80 Feet over either Way. The principal Buildings are the Chapel, the Hall, the Library, and the Mafter's Lodgings. The Chapel and the Hall are fituated on the South Side of the old Quadrangle. Over the Gateway facing the Chapel is an excellent Statue of King *James* II.

The Mafter's Lodgings take up the Eaft and part of the North Side of the new Quadrangle, and is an elegant Building.

Univerfity College is generally faid to be the oldeft Foundation in *Oxford;* that it was erected and endowed by King *Alfred, Anno* 882; but as there are no remains of thofe Halls, faid to be e-

F rected

rected by *Alfred*, and the Students in the Reign of the Conqueror were deprived of their Stipends settled upon them, which used to issue out of the King's Exchequer, and the present College was built and endowed long after *Baliol*, that old Foundation disputes the Point of Antiquity with this. And it appears that the Hall, where this Society performed their Exercises, was from the Conquest 'till the Year 1232 hired by the Students of the Townsmen, of whom *William* Archdeacon of *Durham*, the Founder, bought it about that Time, and gave it to the Scholars of this House, endowing the same with Lands. The same Archdeacon bequeathed 310 Marks for the Education of ten or twelve Students in the University at large, which Money the Vice-Chancellor and Masters at first lent to the Scholars, on Security given for the Re-payment of it. Afterwards four Masters were delegated for the Administration of this Charity, which was laid out in making Purchases of Houses for the Students. The most considerable Benefactors, after the Archdeacon, were *Henry Piercy*, Earl of *Northumberland*; *Robert Dudley*, Earl of *Leicester*; Sir *Simon Bennet*, who in the Year 1638 entirely built the extensive Front of the West Quadrangle, ending at the Bow-window, at his own Expence. The last by whom this College was completed, was Dr. *John Radcliff*; with whose Benefaction the Master's Lodgings, and all the new Building in the Eastern Quadrangle (which includes the Remainder of the Front) was erected: As an Acknowledgment of which, there is a Statue of him in a Niche over the Gateway facing the Master's Garden. The same Gentleman also settled 600 *l. per Annum* on two travelling Fellow-

ships,

fhips, and has indeed been the moſt bountiful Benefactor to the Univerſity in general, that has appeared in the two laſt Centuries.

In this College there are one Maſter, 12 Fellows, 17 Scholars, and uſually about 100 Students of all ſorts. The King is Viſitor.

Late and preſent Maſter,

1728. *Thomas Cockman*, D. D.

1744. *John Browne*, D. D. Vice-Chancellor from *Michaelmas* 1750, to *Michaelmas*, 1753.

✿✿✿✿✿✿✿✿✿✿✿✿✿✿✿✿✿✿✿✿

ALL-SOULS COLLEGE.

THIS College is ſituated in the *High-Street*, Weſt of *Queen*'s, and conſiſts chiefly of two Courts. 1. The old Court is about 124 Feet in Length, and 72 in Breadth, having the *High-Street* on the South, and the Chapel at the North End of it. In this old Quadrangle is a Dial, contriv'd by that ingenious Architect Sir *Chriſtopher Wren*, when Fellow of the College, which, by the help of two Half Rays, and one whole one for every Hour, ſhews to a Minute what is the Time, the Minutes being mark'd on the Sides of the Rays, fifteen on each Side, and divided in fives by a different Character.

2. Their grand Court, ſituated behind the former, is a ſpacious and beautiful Quadrangle, having the Library on the North, the Hall and Chapel on the South, the Cloiſter on the Weſt, and the Common Room, with other handſome Apartments, on the Eaſt, adorned with two beautiful *Gothic* Towers. This Court is in Length from North to South about 172 Feet, and in Breadth

155. The Chapel of this College is about 70 Feet long, and 30 broad; the Anti-Chapel of the same Dimensions; the Altar-Piece is of beautiful clouded Marble, and over it a fine Assumption-Piece of the Founder, painted by Sir *James Thornhill*. Here are also two elegant Vases, one on each Side of the Altar, by the same Hand; the Bas-Relief of which represents the Institution of the two Sacraments.

The Roof of the Chapel is divided into Compartments, carved and gilded. The Screen, which divides the Chapel from the Anti-Chapel, is a neat Piece of Architecture by Sir *Christopher Wren*. In the Anti-Chapel are several Monuments worthy of Notice, particularly those of the Hon. *Doddington Greville* and Dr. *Geo. Clarke*.

The New Library is a magnificent Gallery, 200 Feet long, and 30 broad, and about 40 Feet high, built of white hewn Stone, and finished at a great Expence. The Outside is *Gothic*, in conformity with the rest of the Quadrangle. The Inside consists of two grand Ranges of Bookcases, one above the other, supported by Pilasters of the *Doric* and *Ionic* Orders. The Cieling, and Piers between the Windows, are adorned with most beautiful Stucco-Work, by the ingenious Mr. *Roberts* of this Place. Over the Bookcases are placed interchangeably Vases, and Bustoes of many eminent Persons, formerly Fellows of the Society.

The following is an exact List of the Busts, beginning on the South Side of the West Window, viz.

1. Sir *Anthony Sherley*, Knight, A. B. Count of the Empire, and Embassador from *Schach Abbas* Emperor of *Persia*, to the *Christian* Princes; in the Reign of *James* I. admitted Fellow, 1582.

2. Sir

PART OF ALL SOULS COLLEGE

J. Green Del. e Sculp.

2. Sir *William Petre*, Knight, LL. D. Secretary of State to *Henry* VIII. and *Edward* VI. and Privy Counsellor to Queen *Mary* and Queen *Elizabeth*, 1523.

3. *George Clarke*, LL. D. Secretary of War, and afterwards, in the Reign of Queen *Anne*, one of the Lords of the Admiralty, Secretary to Prince *George* of *Denmark*, and in five Parliaments Burgess for the University, 1680.

4. Sir *Daniel Dunn*, Knight, LL. D. Dean of the Arches, and one of the first Burgesses in Parliament for the University, 1567.

5. *Henry Coventry*, Esq; LL. B. Embassador at *Paris*, and Secretary of State in the Reign of *Charles* II. 1634.

6. Sir *Robert Weston*, Knight, LL. D. Dean of the Arches, and Lord Chancellor of *Ireland*, 1536.

7. Sir *William Trumbul*, Knight, LL. D. Embassador to the *French* and *Turkish* Courts, in the Reign of *James* II. Secretary of State to King *William* III. and Burgess of the University, 1657.

8. *Charles Talbot*, LL. D. Baron of *Hensol*, and Lord High Chancellor of *England*, 1704.

9. Sir *Christopher Wren*, Knight, the famous Architect, LL. D. and Savilian Professor of Astronomy, 1653.

10. *Richard Steward*, LL. D. Dean of St. *Paul*'s, Provost of *Eton*, Clerk of the Closet to *Charles* I. and Commissioner for Ecclesiastical Affairs at the Treaty at *Uxbridge*, 1613.

11. *Thomas Tanner*, D. D. Bishop of St. *Asaph*, 1696.

12. *James Goldwell*, LL. D. Bishop of *Norwich*, and Secretary of State to *Edward* IV. 1441.

13. *Gilbert Sheldon*, D. D. Archbishop of *Canterbury*, and Chancellor of the University, 1622.

14. *Brian Duppa*, D. D. Bishop of *Winchester*, Preceptor to *Charles* II. when Prince of *Wales*, and Lord Almoner, 1612.

15. *David Pole*, LL. D. Dean of the Arches and Bishop of *Peterborough*, 1520.

16. *Jeremy Taylor*, D. D. Bishop of *Down* and *Connor*, 1635.

17. *John Norris*, A. M. Rector of *Bemerton*, *Wilts*, 1680.

18. *Thomas Sydenham*, M. D. 1648.

19. *Thomas Lynaker*, M. D. Founder of the College of Physicians, *London*, 1484.

20. Sir *Clement Edmonds*, Knight, A. M. Secretary of the Council, in the Reign of *James* I. and Burgess for the University, 1590.

21. Sir *William Byrde*, Knight, LL. D. Dean of the Arches and Burgess for the University, 1578.

22. Sir *Nathanael Lloyd*, Knight, LL. D. Judge Advocate and Master of *Trinity Hall* in *Cambridge*, 1689.

23. *Robert Hovenden*, D. D. Warden of *All-Souls*, 1565.

24. Sir *John Mason*, Knight, M. B. Privy Councellor to *Henry* VIII. *Edward* VI. Queen *Mary* and Queen *Elizabeth*, and the first Lay Chancellor of the University of *Oxford*, 1521.

Over the great Door is a very fine Bust of the Founder, Archbishop *Chicheley*, in white Marble, done by Mr. *Roubilliac*. The Elegance of the Room, and the Choiceness of the Collection, consisting greatly of scarce and foreign Books, make this esteemed one of the best Libraries in *Oxford*.

The Statue of that generous Benefactor, Colonel *Godrington*, is erected in the Middle of the Library, on a Pedestal of veined Marble; this Part of the Building being twice the Breadth of the

reſt. It appears, by an Inſcription on the Pede-
ſtal, that the Colonel died *Anno* 1710, and that
the Statue was erected in the Year, 1730. The
Area, or wide Space in the Middle of the Building, divides it in a manner into two Rooms.

The Hall is an elegant Room, in which are
the Portraits of Archbiſhop *Chicheley*, Founder;
Colonel *Codrington*, and Sir *Nathanael Lloyd*. At
the upper End of the Room, under the Founder's Picture, is a Piece of Sir *James Thornhill*'s repreſenting the finding of the Law, and
Joſiah renting his Cloaths, from 2 *King* xxii. 11.
Over the Chimney-piece, which is a very neat
one of Dove-colour'd Marble, is a Buſt of the
Founder, and on one Side of him *Lynaker*, and
on the other *John Leland*, the famous Antiquarian and Author of the Itinerary; who, as Mr.
Hearne informs us, was a Member of this Society. The Room is ornamented with many
other Buſts, which are chiefly Copies from an-
tique Originals.

The College Buttery, which is divided by a
Paſſage from the Hall, is a very pretty Room,
of an oval Form, with an arch'd Stone Roof of
very curious Work.

The Common Room is a very good one, being
a Cube of 26 Feet, and lighted by a large Venetian
Window.

The Warden's Lodgings, which front the
High-Street, and are contiguous to the reſt of the
College, is a handſome Houſe, late the Dwelling
of *George Clarke*, LL. D. a great Benefactor.

The private Apartments of the College are
generally very neat and convenient. The Room
in the old Quadrangle, which was formerly the
Library (before the new one above deſcrib'd was
                                                    finiſh'd)

finiſh'd) is lately fitted up, by one of the Fellows, in a very elegant Manner, in the Gothic Taſte ; and is deſervedly eſteem'd one of the Curioſities of the Houſe.

The Founder of this College, Dr. *Henry Chicheley*, was born at *Higham Ferrers* in *Northamptonſhire*; and having had his School Learning in that Town, was, in the Year 1387, made, by *William* of *Wickham*, one of his firſt Sett of Fellows at *New College* in *Oxford*, where he took the Degree of Doctor of Civil Law. He was made Archdeacon of *Sarum*, and afterwards Chancellor of the ſame Church, by Dr. *Richard Medeford*, Biſhop of that Dioceſe; and becoming known to King *Henry* IV. was ſent on ſeveral Embaſſies by that Monarch, and advanced firſt to the Biſhopric of St. *David*'s, in which having continued five Years, he was tranſlated on *July* 29, 1414, to the See of *Canterbury*, of which he remained Archbiſhop twenty-nine Years. He laid the Foundation of *All-Souls* College in 1437 ; the Charter of Incorporation is dated *May* 20, 16 *Henry* VI. in which it is called *Collegium Animarum omnium Fidelium defunctorum de* Oxon.

By the Statutes he gave this College, he appointed forty Fellows, whereof twenty-four were directed to ſtudy Divinity and Philoſophy, and the other ſixteen the Civil and Canon Law. He procured from King *Henry* VI. a Grant of the Lands and Revenues of ſeveral diſſolved Priories to endow his College, and in his Life-time erected the Chapel, and all the reſt of the Buildings (except ſome very modern ones) which coſt him 4545 *l.* and at his Death gave to the Society the Sums of 134 *l.* 6 *s.* 8 *d.* and 100 Marks.

The moſt conſiderable Benefactors, next to
the

the Founder, have been Colonel *Chriſtopher Co-drington*, Governor of the *Leeward Iſlands*, and Fellow of *All-Souls*, already mentioned, *George Clarke*, LL. D. the late Duke of *Wharton*, *Doddington Greville*, Eſq; Lieutenant General *Stewart*, and Sir *Nathanael Lloyd*, (who at the Time that he was Fellow of this College, was Head of a College in *Cambridge*.) The Colonel bequeathed 6000 *l.* for building the noble Library already deſcribed, his own valuable Study of Books, and 4000 *l.* more to purchaſe new ones; and Dr. *Clarke* gave his beautiful Houſe, &c. for the Uſe of the Wardens ſucceſſively of the College. He alſo very much augmented the Chaplainſhips, and intended to have been a much larger Benefactor to the College, but thought proper to beſtow thoſe Favours on *Worceſter* College.

In this College are one Warden, forty Fellows, two Chaplains, and nine Clerks.

A very peculiar Cuſtom is the celebrating the *Mallard* Night, every Year, on the 14th of *January*, in Remembrance of an exceſſive large *Mallard* or *Drake*, ſuppos'd to have long rang'd in a Drain or Sewer where it was found at the Digging for the Foundation of the College. A very authentic Account of this Event hath lately been retriev'd, and publiſh'd to the learned World, from a Manuſcript of *Thomas Walſingham* the Hiſtorian, and Monk of St. *Albans*. It is the Cauſe of much Mirth, for on the Day, and in Remembrance of the *Mallard*, is always ſung a merry old Song ſet to ancient Muſic.

The Viſitor is the Archbiſhop of *Canterbury*.
Late and preſent Warden.
1702. *Bernard Gardiner*, LL. D.
1726. *Stephen Niblett*, D. D.   B R A-

BRAZEN-NOSE College—

—— F ORMS the Weſt-Side of the *Radcliff* Square. Was founded in the Year 1511 by the joint Benefaction of *William Smith,* Biſhop of *Lincoln,* and *Richard Sutton,* Knight.

The moſt probable Account of the *uncommon Name* of this College ſeems to be this: The Founders purchas'd from *Univerſity* College, for the Scite of their intended Building, two ancient Seats of Learning, *Brazen-Noſe* and little Univerſity Halls; or, as the laſt was more commonly call'd, *Black-Hall.* Both theſe are ſuppos'd to have receiv'd their reſpective Names from ſome Students, who remov'd thither from two ſuch ſeminaries in the temporary Univerſity of *Stamford.* And *Anthony Wood* ſays the *Stamford* Seminary was call'd *Brazen-Noſe* from an Iron Ring fix'd in a Noſe of Braſs ſerving as a Knocker to the Gate; which I believe is remaining there to this Day.

But another Antiquary, Dr. *White Kennet,* ſays that it was originally a *Copper-Noſe,* or a red carbuncled-Noſe, which was commonly expos'd as a Sign to ſome *Hoſpitia,* Inns, or Houſes of Entertainment; and from thence probably, the *Hotel,* or Hall, at *Oxford,* as well as the other at *Stamford,* had its Denomination. (See Gloſs. to Parochial Antiquities in V. Coproſe.)

The Founders, with a View to both theſe ancient Seats of Learning, order'd their new Seminary to be call'd, *The King's Hall and College of Brazen-Noſe.* Agreeable to its Antiquity, as *Univerſity-Hall,* there are ſtill over the Door of the Refectory two very ancient Buſts. The one of the glorious *Alfred* the firſt Founder, the other

of

of *John Erigena* a *Scotchman*, who firſt read Lectures there in the Year 882.

The Refectory itſelf is neat and convenient, adorn'd with the Pictures of the principal Benefactors, and very good Paintings on Glaſs of the two Founders. It ſtands on the South Side of the firſt Quadrangle. In the Center of which is a Statue of *Cain* and *Abel*.

Through a Paſſage on the left Hand of the Gate of the firſt Quadrangle you enter the ſecond. This is a more modern Structure. Though the Stone is mouldring, the Deſign is elegant. And is ſuppos'd to have fallen from the Hands of that great Architect Sir *Chriſtopher Wren*.

A Cloiſter with a Library over it forms the Eaſt Side, the Chapel the South. The Area is diſpos'd in the Form of a Garden planted with flow'ring Shrubs.

The Library is rather calculated for real Uſe than ornamental Shew. The Chapel has a Neatneſs and Simplicity becoming the Houſe of God. If theſe may be conſider'd as the Parents of Beauty, this Edifice has very ſtrong Pretenſions to it. The Roof and Altar-Piece are each reſpectively fine.

The Anti-Chapel has an elegant Monument to the Memory of the late Principal. On this, a maſterly Buſt gives you the ſtrongeſt Features of his Face; an *attic* Inſcription of his Mind.

The Foundation of this College is for one Principal, twenty Fellows, thirty-two Scholars, and four Exhibitioners.

The Number of Names in the Book at preſent are one hundred and ten.

Viſitor

Visitor. The Bishop of *Lincoln*.

1710. Late Principal, *Robert Shippen*, D. D.
1745 Present Principal, *Fr. Yarborough*, D. D.

I proceed in the next Place, to the Description of the three Colleges situated between the new Church of *All-Saints* in the *High-Street*, and the *Turl*, or *Torald* Gate.

These are *Lincoln*, *Exeter* and *Jesus*, which form almost an entire Street alone; there being but few private Houses in it.

❖❖❖❖❖❖❖❖❖❖❖❖❖❖❖❖❖

LINCOLN COLLEGE.

THIS College is situated near *All-Saints* Church, the Front is 210 Feet long. It consists of two Courts. The first we enter through a handsome Portal, with a Tower over it, and is 80 Feet over either Way. The Rector's Lodgings are in the South East Angle, built by *Thomas Beckington*, Bishop of *Bath* and *Wells* about the Year 1465. The South Court is less than the other, 70 Feet square.

The principal Buildings are the Chapel, the Hall, and the Library.

The Chapel, which is on the South Side of the lesser Court, well deserves to be seen; the Screen whereof is Cedar, finely carv'd, and mention'd by Dr. *Plot* as a great Curiosity. It was first built in 1436. by Dr. *Forrest*, Dean of *Wells*, and Prebendary of *Banbury* in the Church of *Lincoln*, and rebuilt by Bishop *Williams*, a great Benefactor. The Windows on the North Side contain Twelve of the Prophets, and those on the South the Twelve Apostles,

Apoſtles, as large as the Life.   Theſe are of old *painted Glaſs* and well preſerv'd.

The Eaſt Window contains the *Types* and *Antitypes* of our *Saviour*; viz. from the North Side 1. the Hiſtory of the Creation, and over it the Nativity of our Saviour.   2. The Paſſing of the *Iſraelites* through the Red Sea, and over it our Saviour's Baptiſm.   3. The *Jewiſh* Paſſover, and over it the Inſtitution of the Lord's Supper.   4. The Brazen Serpent in the Wilderneſs, and⸺ our Saviour on the Croſs.   5. *Jonas* delivered from the Whale's Belly, and⸺our Saviour's Reſurrection. 6. *Elijah* in the fiery Chariot, and⸺ our Saviour's Aſcenſion.   The Cieling which is wainſcotted with Cedar, is imbelliſh'd with the Arms of the Founders and Benefactors of the College, with Cherubims, Palm Branches, Feſtoons, &c. well painted and Gilt.   The lower Cedar Deſks are ornamented with Eight well-executed Figures of the ſame Wood, viz. *Moſes, Aaron,* the Four Evangeliſts, St. *Peter* and St. *Paul.*

The Hall, which is at the upper End of the Great Court oppoſite the Gate, is 40 Feet long, 25 broad, and of a proportionable Heighth.   It was built in 1631. at the Expence of Dr. *John Williams,* Biſhop of *Lincoln.*   And in 1701. was new wainſcotted by the Benefaction of Biſhop *Crewe,* whoſe Arms are plac'd over the Middle of the Screen, as are thoſe of the reſt of the Contributors over other Parts of the Wainſcot.

The Library is a handſome Edifice in the Great Court, over the Common Room.   It has ſeveral valuable Manuſcripts given by *Thomas Gaſcoigne* and others in 1432, and a good Collection of printed Books by ſubſequent Benefactors.   This Room was greatly improv'd in 1662, when

G   Biſhop

Bishop *Crewe* was Rector, at the Expence of *John*
Lord *Crewe* his Father. And in 1738. underwent
a new Change, and was new sash'd and wainscot-
ted by the Benefaction of Sir *Nathanael Lloyd*, first
Commoner of this College, and afterwards Fellow
of *All-Souls* College.

The College was founded by *Richard Flemming*
a Native of *Croyston* in *Yorkshire*, about the Year
1429, who received his Education in this University, where he was first a strenuous Assertor of
Wickliff's Doctrine, and afterwards no less zealous
against it: Insomuch, that it is said he designed
this College as a Seminary for learned Men who
should oppose those Opinions. He was made Bishop of *Lincoln* by King *Henry* V. and died in
the Year 1431. He obtained the Charter of Incorporation from King *Henry* VI. in the 6th Year
of his Reign, whereby he was impowered to annex to it the Rectory of *All-Hallows* adjoining, and
constituted the Rector and Fellows perpetual Pa-
trons of this Church.

And though the Bishop died before he finished
the Design, the Building of the Front or West
Side of the first Quadrangle, was carried on by the
Money he left for that Purpose, and by subsequent
Benefactors; among whom was *William Finden* of
Childry, Esq; and *Thomas Rottherham*, Bishop of
Lincoln, who gave them also a Body of Statutes.
He was translated from *Lincoln* to the See of *York*,
and constituted Lord Chancellor of *England*.

The principal Benefactors are *Richard Flemming*
Bishop of *Lincoln*; *William Daguile*, Gent. May-
or of *Oxford*; *William Smith*, Bishop of *Lincoln*;
Edmund Audley, Bishop of *Sarum*: *Robert Trapp*
of *London*, Gent. *T. Randall*, B. D. Fellow of the
College; *J. Williams*, Bishop of *Lincoln*, and afterwards

afterwards Archbifhop of *York*; *T. Marfhal,* Dean
of *Gloucefter,* and Rector of the College; *John
Southam,* Archdeacon of *Oxford*; and many others.
But *Nathanael* Lord CREWE, late Bifhop of *Durham,* is to be accounted the principal Benefactor,
who making a Vifit here in the Year 1717, after
contributing liberally towards the Buildings at that
time carrying on at *Chrift Church, Queen's, Worcefter,* and *All-Souls,* Colleges, and alfo to the
Univerfity Cheft, gave, by Way of a Rent Charge,
free from Deductions, iffuing out of all his Manors
in the Counties of *Northumberland* and *Durham,*
certain Augmentations to the Rector, Fellows,
Chaplains to the College Churches, Exhibitioners,
Scholars and Bible Clerk; and what enhanc'd the
Merit of his Beneficence, moft of them receiv'd
their Stipends within a few Months; as did the
whole Society foon after, this great and munificent
Benefactor being ftill living.

On the Feafts of St. *Michael* and *All-Saints*
the Society go to Prayers at St. *Michael's* and
All-Saints Churches in Proceffion in their proper
Habits; and a Sermon is preach'd at each Church
by one of the Fellows appointed for that Purpofe.

The Society confifts of a Rector, 12 Fellows,
two Chaplains, 6 Exhibitioners, 6 Scholars, and
a Bible Clerk. The Students of all Sorts about
Fifty.

The Vifitor is the Bifhop of *Lincoln.*

Late and prefent Rector,

1731. *Eufebius Ifham,* D. D.
1755. *Richard Hutchins,* D. D.

JESUS

JESUS COLLEGE.

THE Front of this College is newly beautified and improved, by a very handfome *Ruftic Gateway* and other Additions.

In the firft Court, the Chapel on the North Side, and Hall on the Weft, are neat well proportioned Rooms, the latter having within thefe few Years been much improved by the Addition of a Cieling and other Ornaments done by Mr. *Roberts.*

The inner Court has three Sides uniformly and neatly built (the Hall before mention'd making the fourth Side of this Quadrangle) and on the Weft Side of it over the Common Room, &c. is a fpacious well furnifh'd Library.

In the Principal's Lodgings is a fine Picture of King *Charles* I. at full Length, by *Vandyke,* and in the Library a half Length of King *Charles* II. and fome Original Pieces of Dr. *Hugh Price,* Dr. *Manfell,* Sir *Leoline Jenkins,* &c. Benefactors to the College.

This College was founded by Queen *Elizabeth,* by Charter bearing Date the 27th of *June,* 1571, in the 13th Year of her Reign, for a Principal, eight Fellows, and eight Scholars. The Queen at the Requeft of *Hugh Price,* LL. D. a Native of *Brecknock,* and Treafurer of the Church of St. *David*'s, granted her Royal Charter of Foundation, and a certain Religious Houfe or Cell call'd *Whitehall,* (which before the Diffolution of Monaftries belonging to the Priory of St. *Fridefwide*) for the Scite of the College, together with fuch Timber and other Materials as fhould be wanted for the building of the College, out of her Majefty's Forefts of *Shotover* and *Stow,* with Licence to the College

to

to receive and hold any Lands, Tenements, &c. not exceeding the Sum of one hundred and sixty Pounds yearly Value.

The first Endowment of this College was by Dr. *Hugh Price,* aforesaid, who by Deed bearing Date the last Day of the said Month of *June,* 1571, convey'd to the College by the Stile and Title of *The Principal, Fellows and Scholars of Jesus College, within the City and University of Oxford, of Queen Elizabeth's Foundation,* certain Lands, Messuages and Tenements in the County of *Brecknock,* of the Value of about 160*l. per Ann.* for the Maintenance and Support of a Principal, eight Fellows, and eight Scholars, being the Number limited in the Original Charter of Foundation ; tho' by Charters since granted at different Times, and the Munificence of subsequent Benefactors, the Number of Fellows and Scholars is now more than doubled.

The Building was begun and carried on at the Expence of Dr. *Hugh Price,* who did not live to see any more of it finished than the East Side of the Quadrangle fronting *Exeter* College, and about half the South Side of the said Quadrangle. The rest of this South Side, Westwards, and the West Side comprehending the Hall, Buttery, and Kitchen, and the Rooms over the two latter (which 'till the Buildings that enclose and form the new Quadrangle were erected served for the College Library) together with the North Side, which includes the Chapel, and Principal's Lodgings being afterwards built by Principal *Powel* and Sir *Eubule Thelwall,* partly with the Money bequeathed by Dr. *Hugh Price,* aforesaid, (who by his last Will left 700*l.* to the College) and partly with the Contributions of other Benefactors, and ample Additions of their own. G 3 The

The principal Benefactors after Dr. *Hugh Price*, who may in some measure be call'd the Founder of this originally little Society, were,

1. Sir *Eubule Thelwall*, Knt. Master of the Alienation Office, one of the Masters in Chancery, and Principal of this College; who besides his Contributions towards the Buildings carried on under his Direction and Care, procured a new Charter from King *James* I. extending their Licence in Mortmain to 600 *l. per Ann.* and increasing the Number of Fellows and Scholars from eight to sixteen, and by Powers granted in this Charter to him and other Commissioners, compiled and established an excellent Body of Statutes for the Regulation and good Government of the College.

2. *Francis Mansell*, (third Son of Sir *Francis Mansell*, of *Muddlescombe* in the County of *Glamorgan*, Bart.) D. D. and Treasurer of the Church of *Llandaffe*, *thrice* Principal of *Jesus* College; to whose Munificence and more than Paternal Affection, and *Assiduity* in solliciting Benefactions, supported by the most amiable Qualities, and by his well known Character of Integrity, Piety, and Zeal for the Service of Religion and Promotion of Learning and good Manners, and happily assisted by that Influence which his Birth and Alliances gave him, the College owes almost all the considerable Benefactions it has since receiv'd.

For no sooner was he elected Principal, than he set himself to consider of the most probable Means, of promoting the Interest and Welfare of this College then almost in its Infancy and in a very low Condition, and judging no Method so likely to support and advance it, as that of placing a Person at the Head of it who by his Wealth, Reputation, and Interest was capable of succouring

it

it in that diftrefs'd Condition, (the Eftates convey'd by Dr. *Hugh Price* for the Original Endowment having been ravifhed from it) he foon after
refign'd his Headfhip to make Room for Sir *Eubule
Thelwall* who fucceeded him, and return'd to his
Fellowfhip at *All-Souls* College, before his Year of
Grace there was expired.

About ten Years after, upon the Death of Sir
Eubule Thelwall, (who during his Government
of the College, fully anfwered the Expectations
conceived of him, as is above related) Dr. *Manfell* was again unanimoufly elected Principal, and
from that time made it the whole Bufinefs of his
Life to improve and adorn this College by his
own bright Example (a lively Pattern of all man-
ly and focial Virtues) and by his unwearied Sol-
licitations (in which he met with furprizing Suc-
cefs) to advance and enlarge it both in its Endowments and Buildings, to both which he contributed very largely himfelf both in his Life
Time and at his Death. For he purchafed moft of
the Ground which now makes the inner Court of
the College, and finifhed about half of the North
and South Sides of that Court, which he join'd
in the Form of two Wings to the Weft Side of
the Hall, &c. which his Predeceffor had finifh'd,
and would have compleated the whole Square,
with the Affiftance of his Friends and other well-
difpofed Perfons who had engaged to affift in it,
if the impending Storms which afterwards over-
whelm'd both Church and State, had not at that
Time put a Stop to his great Defigns; fo that the
whole was not completed in the Form in which
it now appears till the Beginning of this Century.

Being afterwards ejected by the Parliament
Commiffioners in 1648 with his whole Society,

(except

(except one Fellow and one Scholar who conde-
scended to comply with the Terms impofed) and
even the College Servants who out of a principle
of Loyalty and Honour, or at leaft out of Refpect
and Affection for their former Mafters, all fhared
the fame Fate ; he notwithftanding continued
with the fame Zeal to promote the Intereft of
his College, procuring feveral Benefactions there-
to even during this Ufurpation ; 'till being in
confequence of the happy Reftoration of the Royal
Family and Government, reftored to his juft
Rights and reinftated in his Headfhip, he within
lefs than a Year after refign'd to open the Way
for a Succeffor, who fhould compleat what he
had long fince begun, and 'till interrupted by the
Publick Troubles, fo happily carry'd on ; and
afterwards to the Time of his Death refided as a
Commoner in the College, over which he had
for many Years fo worthily prefided, (being firft
elected Principal in the Year 1620) and by Will
left his whole Eftate to the College ; an example
of Generofity and publick Spirit hardly to be parallel'd, but furely never to be forgotten !

3. Upon this Refignation, Dr. *Jenkins* was e-
lected Principal (afterwards Sir *Leoline Jenkins*,
Knt. Judge of the Admiralty and Prerogative
Courts, and Secretary of State to King *Charles* II.
and King *James* II. befides other High Offices
and Employments which he fill'd with Reputation
and Dignity, and executed with the greateft Integrity) a Perfon moft happily fitted to reftore
the fhatter'd Conftitution of the College to its
former Vigour, which in the late Times of Con-
fufion had greatly fuffer'd both in its Difcipline
and Revenues. This Gentleman, befides the
eminent Service he did the College in his Life-
time

time by recovering the Revenues of it and re-
forming the Abuſes that had crept into it during
the Intruſion, by his vigilant and prudent Government and his great Reputation, at his Death
bequeath'd his whole Eſtate to the College after
Payment of ſome Legacies, and a few Annui-
ties to ſome of his neareſt Relations and De-
pendants, determinable upon their Deaths reſpectively.

The other Benefactors to this College were,
Dr. *Griffith Lloyd*, Principal; *Herbert Weſtphaling*,
D. D. and Biſhop of *Hereford*; *Henry Rowland*,
D. D. and Biſhop of *Bangor*; Mr. *Owen Wood*,
Dean of *Armagh*; the Rev. Mr. *Thomas Red-
dricke*; *Griffith Powell*, LL. D. and Principal;
Mrs. *Mary Robinſon* of *Monmouth*; *Richard Par-
ry*, D. D. and Biſhop of St. *Aſaph*; the Rev. Mr.
William Prichard; Sir *Thomas Canon*, Knt. *Oliver
Lloyd*, LL. D. and Chancellor of *Hereford*; Sir
Thomas Wynne, Knt. *Stephen Rodway*, Eſq; Sir
John Walter, Knt. *Richard Budde*, Eſq; Serjeant
Owen, Mr. *William Thomas*, King *Charles* I. of
ever bleſſed Memory, (who founded one Fellow-
ſhip in this College, and two more in the Col-
leges of *Exeter* and *Pembroke*, for his Loyal Sub-
jects the Natives of the Iſlands of *Jerſey* and
Guernſey,) *David Parry*, Eſq; Mr. *William Rob-
ſon*, Dr. *Thomas Gwynne*, Precentor of *Sarum* and
Chancellor of *Llandaffe*; *William Backhouſe* of
Swallowfield, in the County of *Berks*, Eſq; *John
Lloyd*, D. D. Biſhop of St. *David*'s and Principal; *Jonathan Edwards*, D. D. and Principal;
Edmund Meyrick, A. M. and Treaſurer of St.
David's and —— *Curre*, Eſq; who moſt of them
ſettled Lands upon the College, or gave Money
to be laid out in the Purchaſe of Lands for the

I   Endow-

Endowment of it: For the Particulars of which we refer to Mr. *Antony Wood's Hist. and Antiq. Universitatis Oxon*, as likewise for a List of Principals, Bishops, and Writers of this College — But besides these there were a very great Number of worthy Benefactors, who, before the College could subsist upon its own *settled* Revenue, (at the Instance of Dr. *Mansell* and other Friends and Favourers of the Design) contributed largely by annual Subscriptions to the Support of the Fellows and Scholars, and to the Advancement of the Buildings then carrying on, whose Names and Benefactions are gratefully recorded in the College Books and Registers.

As there were two Fellowships and two Scholarships founded in Consequence of Sir *Leoline Jenkins's* Will, (one of which Fellowships he directed to be call'd the Fellowship of King *Charles* II. and the other the Fellowship of King *James* II. in grateful Remembrance of the Favours he had receiv'd under those two Princes, which enabled him under God to become a Benefactor to his College and Country;) and one other Fellowship in pursuance of a Decree in Chancery, directing the Application of the remainder of his Personal Estate; the Society now consists of a Principal, 19 Fellows and 18 Scholars, besides a considerable Number of Exhibitioners.

The chief Curiosities in this College, besides those already mentioned, are, 1. a most magnificent Piece of Plate, the Gift of the late Sir *Watkin Williams Wynne*, Bart. for the Use of the Fellows Common Room. And 2. the Statutes of the College written upon Vellum, in the most exquisite Manner, by the Reverend Mr. *Parry* of *Shipston* upon *Stour*, formerly Fellow of this College.   The

The Visitor is the Earl of *Pembroke*.
Late and present Principal.
Eubule Thelwall, D. D.
Thomas Pardo, D. D.

EXETER COLLEGE.

THIS College is situated within the *Turl* Gate,
the Front whereof is 220 Feet long, in the
Center of which is a magnificent Gate and Tower
over it. The Composition of each Front (*viz.*
that towards the Street and that towards the Quadrangle) is a *Rustic Basement* which forms the
Gateway; a *Plinth* whereon are placed four *Pilasters* of the *Ionic* Order, supporting a semicircular *Pediment*, in the *Area* of which are the Founder's Arms on a genteel Shield adorned with Festoons; finishing with a *Balustrade* above all : This,
with the beautiful arched Roof of the Gateway,
is justly esteemed an elegant Piece of Workmanship. The Building within chiefly consists of a
large Quadrangle, formed by the Hall, the Chapel,
the Rector's Lodgings, and the Chambers of the
Fellows and Scholars, and is regular and uniform.

The Gardens are neatly dispos'd, and, tho' within the Town, have an airy and pleasant opening
to the East.

The Library is well-furnish'd with Books in the
several Arts and Sciences; and a very valuable
Collection of the Classicks given by *Edward
Richards*, Esq;

Sir *John Acland* built the Hall in 1618, and Dr.
Hakewill, first Fellow and afterwards Rector,
founded the Chapel in the Year 1624.

The

The Bachelors of Arts and Pupils of this College perform their Determinations, &c. in the House before they enter upon them in the public Schools.

Walter Stapledon, Bishop of *Exeter*, Lord Treasurer of *England*, and Secretary of State to King *Edward* II. 1316, obtain'd a Charter for founding a College where *Hertford* College now stands; but wanting room for the Buildings he designed, he removed his Scholars to the present House, and gave it the Name of *Stapledon-Hall*, after his own Name. He founded a Society consisting of Thirteen, i. e. a Rector and twelve Fellows; one of whom the Chaplain, to be appointed by the Dean and Chapter of *Exeter*; eight to be elected out of the Archdeaconries of *Exeter*, *Totness* and *Barnstaple* in *Devonshire*, and four out of the Archdeaconry of *Cornwall*.

Among the subsequent Benefactors was *Edmund Stafford*, Bishop of *Exeter*, who obtained leave to alter the Name of this House; and settled two Fellowships for the Diocese of *Sarum*. Sir *William Petre* in Queen *Elizabeth*'s Time obtain'd a new Charter and Statutes, founded eight Fellowships for such Counties wherever he then had, or his Heirs at any Time after should have Estates; which by this Time comprehends most of the Counties in *England*. King *Charles* I. added one Fellowship for the Islands of *Jersey* and *Guernsey*. And by Mrs. *Shiers*'s Benefaction, as completed and settled by Dr. *Hugh Shortridge*, two other Fellowships were added, confin'd to the Counties of *Hertford* and *Surry*; besides considerable Augmentations to the Revenues of the College and Society.

The present Members are a Rector, 25 Fellows, one Scholar, who is Bible Clerk, two Exhibitioners:

hibitioners: The whole Number of Members a-
bout an hundred.

The Vifitor the Bifhop of *Exeter*.

Prefent and late Rectors.

1737. *James Edgecumb*, D. D.
1750. *Francis Webber*, D. D.

✿✿✿✿✿✿✿✿✿✿✿✿✿✿✿✿✿✿✿✿✿✿✿✿✿✿

TRINITY COLLEGE.

WIthout the City, oppofite the *Turl*, ftands
Trinity College, the Front whereof is
form'd by the South Side of the Chapel, and the
Tower; under which we enter the firft Court.[26]
This Court is fmall; the South Side is taken up by
the Chapel; the Eaft by the Prefident's Lodgings
and the College Library; the Weft Side by the
Hall and Common Room; and the North by the
Chambers of the Fellows, &c.

The fecond Court is much larger than the firft,
elegantly built of hewn Stone, and fafh'd after
the modern way, confifting of three Sides to the
North, Weft and South; but on the Eaft Side it
lies open to the Garden, from which it is feparated
by an Iron Gate and Palifade. This Court may
be efteem'd one of the Beauties of *Oxford*, not only on account of its Buildings, but as it opens into one of the moft delightful and fpacious Gardens
in Town.[27] It fhould be remember'd that this Court
was one of the firft Specimens of modern Architecture in the Univerfity, and was plann'd by
Sir *Chriftopher Wren*.

The Chapel here is exquifitely finifhed; its

Screen

Screen and Altar-Piece are of Cedar curiously
work'd, and the latter is embellish'd with Carvings
of that eminent Artist Mr. *Guibbons*; the Floor is
laid with black and white Marble; the Cieling
adorn'd with admirable Stucco of a very high Relief, in the middle of which is an *Ascension* finely
painted; and that which appears to be the Frame
round this Picture is a curious *Deceptio Visus*, or
Deception of the Sight; for it does not really
project, but is on a Level with the rest of the
Cieling. In a word, this Chapel is a most perfect Pattern of Elegance join'd with Simplicity.

The Hall is a handsome *Gothick* Room, adorned with the Pictures of their Founder and Benefactors.

The Library was the first Publick One in the
University while it was call'd *Durham College*. In
it is a curious Manuscript, well preserv'd, of *Eu-
clid*, suppos'd to be 600 Years old, which was
translated from the *Arabick* into *Latin* before the
Original *Greek* was found.

The Gardens of this College are large and well
laid out, containing about four Acres of Ground.
The larger Division, which we enter from the
grand Court, consists of fine Gravel-Walks and
Grass-Plots, adorn'd with Evergreens, with which
the Walls likewise are entirely cover'd. At the
lower End of the Center Walk is a beautiful Iron
Gate, supported by two very elegant Piers. This
Gate affords those who pass to and from the Parks
an agreeable Prospect of the Garden and College.
It is remarkable that when the Workmen were
sawing the Stones, in order to build the Piers, in
the Heart of a large Block was found a Toad alive,
which for aught we know, might have been there
ever since the Deluge: But this is a Point to be
                              discuss'd

diſcuſs'd by Naturaliſts ; to whom we leave it. The leſſer Diviſion on the South has been lately laid open to the reſt, planted with flowering Shrubs, and the whole much improv'd

As to the Foundation of this Houſe. it appears that *Durham* College, a ſeminary in *Oxford* for the Education of the Monks of the Cathedral of *Durham,* was diſſolved (with other religious Houſes) in the Reign of *Henry* VIII. Not many Years afterwards, viz. in the Reign of Queen *Mary,* Sir *Tho. Pope*, Kt. of *Titthenhanger* in *Hertfordſhire,* obtained a Charter, dated *March* 8, 1554. to found a College, dedicated to the Holy Trinity, on the Scite of this diſſolv'd Monaſtery ; which he endow'd with a ſuitable Revenue for the Mainte- nance of a Preſident, and twelve Fellows, which are deſtin'd to the Studies of Philoſophy and Divi- nity ; as alſo, for the Maintenance of eight Scholars to be educated in the Studies of Logic, Rhetoric, and the more polite Arts, which are order'd to be choſen (after due Trial) out of thoſe Manors which were in the Poſſeſſion of the Founder at the Time of his erecting this College ; but if none appear'd from the aforeſaid Manors on the Day of Election, viz. *Trinity Monday*, the Preſident and Fellows are directed to ſupply the Vacancies from any other Part of *England.* It is order'd likewiſe that no more than two Natives of the ſame Coun- ty ſhould be Fellows of this College at the ſame Time ; *Oxfordſhire* being excepted, of which County there may be Five. The Founder after- wards granted other Lands for the Maintenance and Education of four other Scholars on the Footing of the former Eight ; that the Number of the Scholars might *correſpond* (as himſelf ex- preſſes it in his Statutes) to that of the Fellows.

The

The principal Benefactor to this College was Dr. *Bathurst*, formerly Prefident, who expended 1900 *l.* in building their beautiful Chapel, and erected the North and Weft Sides of their new Court.

The prefent Members of this fociety are a Prefident, twelve Fellows and twelve Scholars abovemention'd. Here are likewife about three Exhibitions ; the moft confiderable of which is that given by Mr. *Tylney* of *Hants*. The whole Number of Students of all Sorts is about Eighty.

The Vifitor is the Bifhop of *Winchefter*.

Late and prefent, Prefident.

1705. *William Dobfon*, D. D.
1731. *George Huddesford*, D. D.

B A L I O L L College.

B A L I O L L College is fituated without the North Gate, a little to the Weftward of *Trinity*, and confifts chiefly of one Court, which we enter by a handfome Gate with a Tower over it. The Buildings about this Court are ancient, except the Eaft End, which is well finifhed with Stone and fafhed after the modern Way ; and the reft of the College is intended to be made equal to it.

The Chapel ftands at the North-Eaft Angle of the great Court. The Hall is at the Weft End of the fame Court. The Mafter's Lodgings is a convenient Apartment, and has fome good Rooms in it, particularly a fpacious Hall, having a large well-preferved ancient Window to the Eaft; and their Library is well-furnifhed with a large Collection

lection of useful Books, and many of the moft ancient Manuscripts.

Over the Gate of the College are the Arms of the *Baliol* Family.

And on the outfide, over-againft the Mafter's Lodgings, is a ftone plac'd Edge-ways, in Memory of thofe learned and pious Prelates, Archbifhop *Cranmer*, Bifhop *Ridley*, and Bifhop *Latimer*, who were burnt at that Place for oppofing the Popifh Religion.[28]

Sir *John Baliol*, of *Bernard* Caftle in *Yorkfhire*, Father of *John Baliol*, King of *Scotland*, is faid to have firft defigned the Foundation of this College for the Education of poor Scholars, on whom he fettled yearly Exhibitions till he could provide them an Houfe; and dying before he purchafed one, he recommended the Defign to his Widow and Relict *Dervorguilla*, Daughter of *Alexander* III. King of *Scotland*, who firft fettled thefe Exhibitions on a Houfe fhe hired of the Univerfity in *Horfemonger-Street*, and in 1284 fhe purchafed of *Thomas D'Ewe*, a Tenement for her *Scholars of Baliol*, and conveyed it, with three Acres of Land, to the Mafter and Scholars of this Houfe for ever, for their Habitation, having obtained a Royal Charter for that Purpofe. She afterwards added feveral new Buildings to it, and fettling other Lands for the Maintenance of the Scholars, dedicated her Foundation to the Honour of the Holy Trinity, the Bleffed Virgin, and St. *Katherine* the Martyr; which Benefactions were afterwards ratified by her Son *John Baliol*, King of *Scotland*, and *Oliver* Bifhop of *Lincoln*, in whofe Diocefe *Oxford* then was. The Value of the Lands and Revenues, belonging to this College, not exceeding 27 *l.* 9 *s.* 4 *d. per Ann.* at that Time; but their

Revenues

Revenues were foon after greatly enlarged by the Benefactions of others, particularly Sir *Philip Somerville*, a Gentleman in *Staffordſhire*, granted to this College the Impropriation of the Pariſh of *Mickle-Benton* in the County of *Northumberland*, with other Lands; and Dr. *John Warner*, Biſhop of *Rocheſter*, founded four *Scotiſh* Exhibitions, endowing them with a Revenue of 20 *l. per Annum* each.

John Snell, Eſq; gave the Manor of *Uffton* in *Warwickſhire* for the Uſe of *Scots* Exhibitioners.

The Paintings on the Windows in the Chapel are deemed curious.

The Members of this Society are at preſent a Maſter, twelve Fellows, fourteen Scholars and eighteen Exhibitioners; the whole Number of Students of all Sorts amounting to about 100.

The Maſter and Fellows elect their Viſitor.

Their late Viſitor was the Rev. Sir *John Dolben*, Bart. who reſigned in 1755. and recommended the Rev. Sir *William Bunbury*, Bart. as his Succeſſor, who was accordingly elected.

Late and preſent Maſter.

1722. *Joſeph Hunt*, D. D.

1727. *Theophilus Leigh*, D. D. Vice-Chancellor in 1738.

St. *JOHN*'s College ——

——IS ſituated North of *Balioll*, in the pleaſant Street of St. *Giles*'s; having a Terraſs, with a Row of tall Elms before it.

The

The Buildings of this College chiefly confift of two large Quadrangles. We enter the firft by a handfome old Gateway with a Tower over it. It is formed by the Hall and Chapel on the North, the Prefident's Lodgings on the Eaft, and the Chambers of the Fellows, Scholars, and other Students on the South and Weft Sides. The Hall is efteemed one of the moft elegant in the Univerfity; being well-proportioned, handfomely wainfcotted and floor'd, and having a beautiful arch'd Roof, a Screen of Portland Stone, and a grand variegated Marble Chimney-Piece, containing a Picture of St. *John* the Baptift, by *Titian*. It is likewife adorned with many other Pictures; viz. at the upper End, by a whole-length Portrait of the Founder; on his Right Hand one of Archbifhop *Laud*, and on his Left one of Archbifhop *Juxon*. On the North and South Sides of the Room are thofe of Bifhop *Mew*, Bifhop *Buckridge*, Sir *William Paddy*, Knight, and other eminent Men who have been Members of, and Benefactors to this Society.

North of the Hall is an excellent *Common Room*; being handfomely wainfcotted, having a Chimney-Piece of Dove-colour'd Marble, and a Cieling curioufly adorned with Compartments and Shell-work in *Stucco* by Mr. *Roberts*.

The Chapel, which is adjoining to the Hall, is in all Refpects neat and commodious. It is divided from the Anti-Chapel by a well-built Screen of Wainfcot in the Corinthian Order, regularly feated, paved with black and white Marble, adorned with handfome Brafs Sconces, and two very beautiful Branches. The Altar is likewife of the Corinthian Order, and very properly adapted. Over the Communion Table is a fine Piece of Tapeftry, reprefenting our Saviour with the two Difciples at

I

Emmaus,

Emmaus, copied from a Painting of *Titian*. On the North Side, in a Recefs, is a large old Organ; and in this Chapel is performed Cathedral Service twice a Day. We muft not omit obferving, that here, and in the Veftry adjoining, are feveral curious Monuments.

Through a Paffage on the Eaft Side of the firft Quadrangle we enter the fecond; on the Eaft and Weft Sides whereof are handfome *Piazzas* in the *Grecian* Tafte, each Column confifting of one fingle bluifh kind of Stone, dug, as we apprehend, upon a Part of the College Eftate near *Fyfield* in *Berkfhire*. In the Center of each *Piazza* is a magnificent Gateway, confifting principally of two Orders, 1. The *Doric*, which forms the Gateway itfelf, agreeable to that of the Piazzas. 2. The *Ionic*, which fupports a Semicircular Pediment. Between four of thefe Columns, *viz.* two on each Side, in a Niche, is a Brafs Statue; that on the Eaft of King *Charles* I. and that on the Weft of his Queen. That neither of the *Greek* Orders might be wanting, the 3d, *viz.* the *Corinthian*, is very artfully introduced in the Conftruction of the Niche. The whole is richly embellifh'd, and is the Defign of that celebrated Architect *Inigo Jones*.

The Library, which includes the upper Story of the South and Eaft Sides, is inferior to few in this Place, tho' not of fo modern a Fafhion as fome. The firft Side is well ftor'd with printed Books in all Faculties, regularly difpos'd and exactly catalogu'd; which is owing to the Pains and Care of the prefent worthy Prefident, who fpent a confiderable Time in effecting it. The fecond with a moft valuable Collection of Manufcripts. As the Book-Cafes of the latter adhere to the Sides, and are not

rang'd

rang'd in Stalls as thofe in the former are, it forms a beautiful and fpacious Gallery. Here likewife are fome valuable Curiofities, particularly the famous Picture of King *Charles* I. which has the whole Book of Pfalms written in the Lines of the Face and the Hair of the Head.

The Gardens belonging to this College are extremely agreeable, very extenfive, and well laid out. They ftill retain the Names they formerly had, when they had nothing to boaft of but a Plantation of tall Elms, *viz.* the *outer* and *inner Grove*. But now the outer one is difpos'd in regular Walks and Grafs-Plats, the Walls thereof cover'd with Evergreens and neatly cut, and is finely fhaded by Trees of various Kinds, *viz.* the middle Walk thereof by a Row of Lime-Trees on each Side cut arch-wife, a Row of cut Elms by the Side-Walks, and at each End and acrofs the middle two Groups of beautiful Horfe-Chefnut-Trees. The inner Grove is of quite a different Caft to this, being fo contriv'd as not to fatiate the Eye at once, but its various Parts prefent themfelves gradually to view. No Spot whatever is calculated to yield a more pleafing Variety; for, except Water, it has all that could be wifh'd.

This College was founded by Sir *Thomas White*, Alderman and Merchant-Taylor of *London*, *Anno* 1555, (1 and 2 *Philip* and *Mary*;) and afterwards re-founded by him, *Anno* 1557. He endow'd it with feveral confiderable Manors, and at his Death bequeathed the Sum of 3000*l.* to purchafe Lands to increafe the Revenues of it. He originally defign'd *Merchant-Taylors* School in *London* for the chief Seminary of his College; but being a Man of a more public Spirit than to confine himfelf to any one Place, he allow'd two Fellowfhips to the City

of

of *Coventry*, two to *Briſtol*, two alſo to the Town of *Reading*, and one to *Tunbridge*.

The moſt conſiderable Benefactors ſince, have been Sir *William Paddy*, who founded and endowed the Choir, and built that Side of the new Quadrangle, of which the Library is a Part. Archbiſhop *Laud*, who at the Expence of above 5000 *l.* (excluſive of 400 *l.* for the Statues of the King and Queen, and 200 Ton of Timber which he obtained by Warrant from *Shotover Foreſt* and *Stow* Wood) added the other three Sides. Archbiſhop *Juxon*, who gave 7000 *l.* to this College; Dr. *Gibbons*, who bequeathed the perpetual Advowſon of the Living of *Baynton* in *Yorkſhire*, and 1000 *l.* to buy Books; Dr. *Holmes*, the late worthy Preſident, with his Lady, who gave 15000 *l.* to augment the Salaries of the Officers, and other Uſes; and Dr. *Rawlinſon*, who bequeathed a conſiderable Number of Books, and the Reverſion of an Eſtate in Fee-Farm Rents.

The preſent Members are a Preſident, fifty Fellows, two Chaplains, an Organiſt, five Singing-Men, ſix Choriſters, and two Sextons. The Number of Students of all Sorts being uſually about eighty.

The Viſitor is the Biſhop of *Wincheſter*.

Late and preſent Preſident.

1728 *William Holmes*, D. D.
1748 *William Derham*, D. D.

WADHAM

❀❀❀❀❀❀❀❀❀❀❀❀❀❀❀❀❀

WADHAM College.

*W*ADHAM College is situated without the City, in that Part of the Suburb called *Holy-well*. It consists chiefly of one grand Quadrangle, and another very small Court within it. The Front of the College is almost opposite to *Trinity* Gardens, having a large Gate, with a Tower over it, by which we enter the great Quadrangle, being near 130 Feet either Way.

The Chapel is a spacious Edifice, at the North-East Angle of the great Court. What is most admired here is a very large Window of painted Glass, at the East End, of the Passion of our Saviour, wherein there are a great Variety of Figures admirably done. This was put up in the Reign of King *James* I. and is said to have cost 1500 *l.* The Windows on the Sides seem to be of the same Workmanship; but the greatest Curiosity in this Chapel is the painted Cloth, if it may be so call'd, at the lower Part of the Altar. It is the only Work of its kind at present in *Oxford*, but the Altar of *Magdalen* College, before the new Wainscotting of it, was done in the same Manner. The Cloth itself, which is of an Ash-Colour, is the Medium; the Lines and Shades are done with a brown Crayon, and the Lights with a white one; which being afterwards pressed with hot Irons, causing the Sweat of the Cloth to incorporate with the Colours, has so fixed them, as to be render'd Proof against a Brush, or any such Thing, made use of to cleanse it from Dust: It was performed by *Isaac Fuller*, who

who painted the Altar-Piece at *Magdalen* College, and is generally allow'd to be masterly Drawing. The East represents the *Lord's Supper*; the North *Abraham* and *Melchisedeck*; and the South the Children of *Israel* gathering *Manna*.

The Hall is situated at the South-East Angle of the great Court. The Library is a lofty spacious Room over the Kitchen, well furnish'd with Books.

The Chapel and the Library form two Wings in the Back or East Front of the College. Between these is a Cloister; and, over that, the Fellows Common Room; which is a very handsome one, and has the Advantage of a beautiful Prospect over the adjacent Fields to *Heddington-Hill*.

This College was design'd by *Nicholas Wadham*, Esq; and founded, in pursuance of his Will, by *Dorothy Wadham*, his Widow, *Anno* 1613, who appointed one Warden, 15 Fellows, 15 Scholars, two Chaplains, two Clerks, one Manciple, two Cooks, two Butlers, and a Porter; the Warden to be a Native of *Great Britain*, but to quit the College on his Marriage, or Advancement to a Bishopric. The Fellows, after having compleated 18 Years from their Regency, to quit their Fellowships. The Scholars, out of whom the Fellows are to be chosen, to be taken three out of *Somersetshire*, and three out of *Essex*; the rest out of any County in *Great Britain*.

The most considerable Benefactor, since the Founder, was *John Goodridge*, M. A. some time Fellow of this College, who gave all his Lands at *Walthamstowe* in *Essex*, to this Society. Dr. *Hoddy* added ten Exhibitions, four for Students in *Hebrew*, and six for *Greek*, 10 *l.* a Year to each. Lord *Wyndham*

ham 2000 *l.* 1500 *l.* to increase the Warden's Salary, and 500 *l.* to beautify and repair the College. Bishop *Lisle*, the late Warden, gave two Exhibitions of 10 *l. per Ann.* each.

The present Members of this Society are a Warden, 15 Fellows, 2 Chaplains, 15 Scholars, two Clerks, and 16 Exhibitioners; the whole Number of Students being usually about 120.

The Visitor is the Bishop of *Bath* and *Wells.*

Late and present Warden.

1739. *Samuel Lisle*, D. D. Bishop of *Norwich.*
1745. *George Wyndham*, D. D.

CORPUS-CHRISTI COLLEGE.

CORPUS-Christi College is in St. *John*'s Parish, between *Christ-Church* on the West, *Merton* College on the East, and *Oriel* College on the North; consisting of one Quadrangle, an elegant Pile of modern Buildings, in which are pleasant and commodious Rooms (that look into *Merton* and *Christ-Church* Meadows) and a Cloyster adjoining; also a neat Structure which looks Eastward towards *Merton* College Grove, in which are six Apartments appropriated to Gentlemen-Commoners, whose Number the Founder has confin'd to Six, who are to be Sons of Noblemen, or other eminent Persons.

On the East Side of the Quadrangle is the Hall, which is 50 Feet long, and 25 broad, and of a proportionable Height.

I

The

The *Cylindrical* Dial in the Quadrangle is set at Right Angles with the *Horizon*, the common Sections whereof, with the Hour Circles, except the *Meridian* Circle that divides it by the *Axis*, as also the *Equinoctial*, are all Ellipses, and is a fine old Piece of *Gnomonicks*. In the Library is a MS. explaining every Part of its Construction.

The Chapel, which is situated at the South-East Corner of the Quadrangle, is 70 Feet in Length, and 25 in Breadth.

The Library is well furnished with Books, particularly a large Collection of Pamphlets from the Reformation to the Revolution. About 300 MSS. An *English* Bible, supposed to be older than *Wickliffe*'s. A Parchment Roll, containing the Pedigree of the Royal Family, and the several Branches of it, from King *Alfred* to *Edward* VI. with their Arms blazoned, signed by the Kings at Arms ; and several other Curiosities, particularly an ancient Manuscript History of the Bible in *French*, finely decorated with curious Paintings, given by General *Oglethorpe*, who was a Member of the College.

They shew here also the genuine Crosier of the Founder, a Piece of very curious Workmanship, little impaired by Time.

This College was founded in the Year 1516, by Dr. *Richard Fox*, a Native of *Ropesley*, near *Grantham* in *Lincolnshire*, who was successively Bishop of the Sees of *Exeter*, *Bath* and *Wells*, *Durham* and *Winchester*, and was likewise Lord Privy Seal to King *Henry* VII. and *Henry* VIII. He first intended it only as a Seminary for the Monks of the Priory, or Cathedral Church of St. *Swithen* at *Winchester*, and obtained a Charter for that End ; but altered his Mind by the Per-

suasion

fuafion of *Hugh Oldham*, Bifhop of *Exeter*, who engaged to be a Benefactor to the Houfe, on condition that he would convert it into a College for the Ufe of fecular Students, after the Manner of other Colleges in the Univerfity: Whereupon Bifhop *Fox* caufed the firft Charter to be cancelled, and obtained another, whereby he was permitted to found a College for the Study of Divinity, Philofophy, and other liberal Arts. The Charter of Foundation was dated at the Caftle of *Wolvefly*, on the Calends of *March* 1516.

He affigned a Body of Statutes for the Government of this Society, whereby he appointed, that the Fellows fhould be elected out of the Scholars, who are to be chofen from the Counties or Diocefes following, *viz.* two *Surrey*, three *Hampfhire*, one *Durham*, two *Bath* and *Wells*, two *Exeter*, two County of *Lincoln*, two *Gloucefterfhire*, one *Wiltfhire*, or (in Defect of a Candidate) the Diocefe of *Sarum*, one County of *Bedford*, two County of *Kent*, one County of *Oxford*, one *Lancafhire*.

Among the Benefactors were *Hugh Oldham*, Chaplain to *Margaret* Countefs of *Richmond*, and afterwards Bifhop of *Exeter*, who gave 6000 Marks towards the Building of this College, befides feveral Eftates for the Endowment of it.

William Froft gave Lands for the Maintenance of one Scholar. *John Claymond*, the firft Prefident of this College, gave Lands at feveral Villages near *Oxford*, and in *Hampfhire*, *Berkfhire*, and other Parts of the Kingdom. *Robert Morwent*, fecond Prefident, gave to the College *Rewley* Meadows near *Oxford*. And in 1706, Dr. *Turner*, when Prefident, gave the New Buildings and his Collection of Books.

The prefent Members of this Society are a Prefident, 20 Fellows, 2 Chaplains, 20 Scholars, and four Exhibitioners; the whole Number of Students being above fixty.

The Bifhop of *Winchefter* is Vifitor.

Late and prefent Prefident.

1715. *John Mather*, D D.
1748. *Thomas Randolph*, D. D.

✽✽✽✽✽✽✽✽✽✽✽✽✽✽✽✽✽✽✽ ✽✽✽✽✽✽✽✽✽

MERTON COLLEGE.

MERTON College is fituated Eaft of *Corpus Chrifti*, and confifts of three Courts. The largeft, or inner Court, is about 110 Feet long, and 100 broad.

The Chapel is at the Weft End of the firft Court, and is likewife St. *John*'s Parifh Church. This is one of the largeft and beft proportion'd Gothic Structures in the Univerfity, 100 Feet in Length, and 30 in Breadth, and has a very capacious Tower and Anti-Chapel. It has lately been clean'd and ornamented. But altho' large at prefent, yet there are evident Tokens of its having been a much larger Church: For what remains appears to have been only the Chantry and Crofs-Ifle; the Nave and Side Ifles being taken away, and the Arches, which led into them, filled up. On the Outfide next to *Corpus Chrifti* this is very difcernible. It is not improbab.e, however, that the Form it now retains ferved as a Model for *New* College, *All-Souls*, and *Magdalen* College Chapels.

In

In the Chapel are the Monuments of Sir *Tho. Bodley*, and Sir *Henry Saville*. In the Anti-Chapel, near the North Door, is a small Inscription to the Memory of Mr. *Anthony Wood*, that diligent Antiquarian. And near the Entrance into the Chapel is the elegant little Monument of Dr. *Wyntle* and his Sister.

The Hall is between the first and the inner Court; and the Library in the small old Quadrangle, South of the Chapel, which is well furnished with ancient and modern Books and Manuscripts.

The Gardens are very pleasant, having the Advantage of a Prospect of the adjacent Country, from the South Terrass.

This Society was first placed at *Malden* in *Surrey* by *Walter de Merton*, Lord Chancellor of *England*, and afterwards Bishop of *Rochester*, *Anno* 1264; but he afterwards removed them from *Malden* to St. *John Baptist*'s Street in *Oxford*, having built a College on some Ground he purchased there. He afterwards established them by a Charter he obtained of the Crown in the Year 1274, endowing it with a suitable Revenue.

With so much Prudence was this College founded, that King *Henry* III. recommended it to *Hugo*, Bishop of *Ely*, as a Model for his intended Munificence in *Cambridge*, according to which *Peter-House* was afterwards erected in that University. And farther, it is said of the Founder of *Merton* College, that tho' in Expence he was the Founder of only one, by Example he was the Founder of many Colleges.

This was the first College in *Oxford* that was incorporated by a Royal Charter, tho' *Baliol* was the first indowed with Lands; for if *University-*

Hall

Hall was indowed by King *Alfred*, it was only at Pleasure, by a Revenue he assigned the Society out of the Exchequer, which was taken away by *William* the Conqueror.

Among the Benefactors were *John Willyott*, S. T. P. Chancellor of the University, who, about *Anno* 1380. gave all his Personal, and Part of his Real Estate, for the Maintenance of certain Exhibitioners, who were afterwards called Postmasters. The Number was then 12, when *John Chambers*, Fellow of *Eton*, and once Fellow of this College, gave 1000 l. *Anno* 1604. to purchase Estates for two additional Ones, to be sent from *Eton* School.

Besides these, there are now four other Scholarships founded by Mr. *Henry Jackson*, late of this College.

In the Election of a Warden, the Fellows chuse three Persons, whom they present to their Visitor, the Archbishop of *Canterbury*, who appoints one of them.

The present Members are a Warden, 24 Fellows, 14 Postmasters, 2 Chaplains, and 2 Clerks; the whole Number of Students of all Sorts being about 100.

Late and present Warden.

1734. *Robert Wyntle*, M. D.
1750. *John Robinson*, D. D.

✳✳✳✳✳✳✳✳✳✳✳✳✳✳✳✳✳✳✳✳✳✳✳✳

ORIEL COLLEGE.

ORIEL College is situated between St. *Mary* Hall on the North, *Corpus Christi* College on the South, and *Christ Church* on the West;

the

the Entrance is oppofite to the Back-Gate of the latter. It chiefly confifts of one regular, uniform, well built Quadrangle. On the North Side whereof is the Library and the Provoft's Lodgings; on the Eaft the Hall, Buttery, and the Entrance into the Chapel, which runs Eaftward from thence; and on the South and Weft Sides are the Chambers of the Fellows and other Students.

Oppofite to the Great Gate we afcend by a large flight of Steps, having a Portico over them, to the Hall; which is a well-proportioned Room as to Length and Breadth, handfomely wainfcotted, with a Doric Entablature, and adorned with three whole-length Portraits, *viz.* in the Middle at the Upper-End, a very fine one of King *Edward* II. enthroned with his *Regalia*, by *Hudfon*; on his Right-Hand, one of Queen *Anne*, by *Dahl*; and on his Left, one of the late Duke of *Beaufort*, by *Soldi*. His Grace is drawn erect in his Parliament Robes, having a Negro Servant bearing his Coronet after him. The whole makes a very fuperb Appearance.

The Chapel is alfo very decently and properly fitted up.

Through a Paffage in the North Side we enter the Garden Court: Which, confidering it is furrounded by the adjacent Buildings, is very fpacious and makes an agreeable Appearance. The Garden is fenced at this End with a Pair of Iron Gates and Palifades, properly fupported by a Dwarf-Wall and Stone Piers. On either Hand is a Wing of new Building, in a Style conformable to the Quadrangle. That on the Right, containing four Sets of Rooms, befide the Garrets, was built at the Expence of Dr. *Robinfon*,

Bifhop

Bifhop of *London:* And that on the Left, at the Expence of Dr. *Carter*, late Provoft; Part whereof being intended as an Addition to the Provoft's Lodgings.

This College was founded by King *Edward* II. 1327. King *Edward* III. and *Adam le Brome*, Almoner to King *Edward* II, who was the firft Provoft, were confiderable Benefactors to this College. King *Edward* III. particularly gave them the large Meffuage of *Le Oriel*, fituate in St. *John's* Parifh, by which Name the College was afterwards called; from whence this College has been frequently held to be a Royal Foundation; but the firft Grant was made to St. *Mary Hall*, from whence the Fellows removed to *Oriel*, after that Houfe was affigned to them. He likewife gave them the Hofpital of St. *Bartholomew* near *Oxford*, with the Lands thereunto belonging; which is inhabited, at prefent, by 8 poor Men, who have a weekly Allowance from the College.

Other Benefactors were *John Frank*, Mafter of the Rolls in the Reign of King *Henry* VI. who gave 1000*l.* to this College at his Death, to purchafe Lands for the Maintenance of four Fellows; *John Carpenter*, once Provoft, and afterwards Bifhop of *Worcefter*, was another Benefactor; as was alfo *William Smith*, Bifhop of *Lincoln*, and *Richard Dudley*, fometime Fellow, and afterwards Chancellor of the Church of *Sarum:* The laft of thefe gave the College the Manor of *Swaynfwick* in *Somerfetfhire*, for the Maintenance of two Fellows and fix Exhibitioners. Queen *Anne* annexed a Prebend of *Rochefter* to the Provoft for ever, to increafe his Income. Dr. *Robinfon*, Bifhop of *London*, befides the New Building, gave 2500*l.* to augment the Fellowfhips.

I   And

And the late Duke of *Beaufort* gave 100 *l. per Ann.* for four Exhibitioners.

The prefent Members are a Provoft, 18 Fellows, and 14 Exhibitioners; the whole Number of Students of all Sorts being about 70.

The Vifitor is the Lord Chancellor.

Late and prefent Provoft.

1708. *George Carter*, D. D.
1728. *Walter Hodges*, D. D.

✿✿✿✿✿✿✿✿✿✿✿✿✿✿✿✿✿✿✿✿✿✿✿✿✿✿✿✿

CHRIST CHURCH.

THIS College merits the Obfervation of Strangers, if we regard either the Dimenfions of its Buildings, the Revenues, or the Number of Students belonging to it. It is fituated in *Fifh-Street*, confifting of four Courts or Squares, *viz.* 1. The great Quadrangle, 2. *Peckwater* Square, 3. *Canterbury* Court; and 4. The Chaplains, befides feveral other leffer Courts.

The Weft Front of the great Quadrangle is a magnificent *Gothic* Building, 382 Feet in length, flanked at each End with two Turrets. The great Gate is in the Middle of this Front, and over it a beautiful Tower, enriched with *Gothic* Ornaments, defigned by Sir *Chriftopher Wren*, erected by Dr. *Fell*, and admirably correfponds to the Tafte of the reft of the Buildings. In this Tower hangs the great Bell, called *Tom*, on the Sound whereof, at Nine at Night, the Scholars of the Univerfity are to retire to their refpective Colleges. Tho' the Windows in the Front are not exactly regular, yet fuch are the Greatnefs of the Proportions, and the Magnificence of the Whole,

that

that they raife the Admiration of every Spectator, and help him to form an Idea of the great Soul of Cardinal W O L S E Y. In this Quadrangle are the Statues of Cardinal *Wolfey*, and Dean *Fell*; that of the Cardinal in the South-Eaft Corner is juftly admired as an excellent Piece of Workmanfhip.

The great Quadrangle is 264 by 261 Feet in the Clear. The Buildings are regular and uniform; only the Hall, which takes up more than half the South Side, is confiderably elevated above the reft, and the whole finifhed with a Baluftrade of Stone. In the Center of the Area, below the Terrafs, is a large Bafon and Fountain adorned with a Statue of *Mercury*, on a Pedeftal erected upon a Foundation of Rock-work.

The Eaft and North Sides of this Quadrangle are taken up with the Dean's and four of the Canons Lodgings. Thefe Lodgings are capacious, for the moft Part elegantly fitted up, and have beautiful Gardens behind them.

In the Year 1638 the North Side of the grand Quadrangle was begun; but, before the Shell was well finifhed, the Civil Wars broke out, whereupon it was demolifhed by the Rebels, and the Timber ferved the Soldiers for Fuel: But, on the Reftoration, this Part of the Building was begun again, by the Direction and Encouragement of Dr. *Fell*, then Dean of the College; and finifhed *Anno* 1665, together with that grand Stair-cafe leading up to the Hall.

The Hall is by far the moft magnificent Room of the Kind in *Oxford*, and perhaps one of the largeft in the Kingdom. The Roof is framed of Timber curiously wrought, and withal fo artfully contrived, as to produce a very grand and

noble

noble Effect. There are near 300 Compartments in the Cornice, which are embellished with
as many Coats of Arms carved and blazoned in
their proper Colours.

At the upper End of the Hall there is an Ascent
of three Steps which run the whole Breadth, al-
lotted to the high Table. Near which is a beautiful Gothic Window in a Recess, that demands
the Attention of the curious Observer.

This superb Room has lately been much beautified, and improved by compleating and painting
the Wainscot, painting and gilding the Roof, and
by the Addition of a great Number of Portraits
of former Deans, of Bishops and other great Men
that were bred at the College, which are disposed
round the Room.

At the upper End hang the Pictures of

King *HENRY* VIII.
in the Middle.

Right Hand.	Left Hand.
Cardinal WOLSEY.	Dean *Fell*, Bp of *Oxford*.
Dean *Duppa*, Bishop of *Winchester*.	Dr. *Morley*, Bp of *Winchester*.
Dr. *King*, Bp of *London*.	Dr. *Boulter*, Dean, and Abp of *Armagh*.
Dr. *Compton*, Bishop of *London*.	Dean *Corbett*.

And on the Sides, Dr. *East*, Bishop of *Cork*. Dr.
Dolben, Abp of *York*. Dr. *Blackbourne*, Abp of
York. Dr. *Hooper*, Bp of *Bath* and *Wells*. Bishop
Wood. Sir *Jonathan Trelawney*, Bp of *Winchester*.
Mr. *John Locke*. Dr. *Benson*, Bp of *Gloucester*, &c.

At the lower End.

Lord *Arlington*. Sir *Dudley Carleton*. Dr. *Ellis*,
　Bishop of *Waterford*.

The

The Cathedral Church serves as a Chapel to the College. The Eaſt Window whereof, which was done by Mr. *Price* Senior of *London*, after a Deſign of Sir *James Thornhill*, repreſents the *Epiphany*. In the *Dormitory*, which is an Iſle on the North Side of the Choir, is the Tomb of St. *Frideſwide*; who died A. D. 739. In the ſame Place, likewiſe, is a Window, curiouſly painted, repreſenting St. *Peter* deliver'd out of Priſon by the *Angel*; beſide the principal Figures there are a conſiderable Number of *Roman* Soldiers in various ſleeping Attitudes, admirably well drawn: And, tho' a very ſmall Portion of the Glaſs is ſtain'd, the Colours are brilliant, and the whole appears very lively. It was painted by *J. Oliver*, in his Eightieth Year, and given by him to the College, in the Year 1700. In this and other Parts of the Church are ſome Monuments, no leſs remarkable for their elegant Inſcriptions, than their beautiful Structure.

In the Tower are ten celebrated Bells.

Three Sides of *Peckwater* Court are uniform, deſign'd by Dr. *Aldrich*, then Dean, no leſs famous for his Skill in Architecture, than for his Eminence in moſt other Branches of Knowledge. Each Side contains 15 Windows in Front. The lower Story is *Ruſtic*, in which are three Entrances. The ſecond Story, and the *Attic* above it are contain'd in the height of the *Ionic* Order, which reſts upon the *Ruſtic*. Over the five middle Windows in each Side is a beautiful Pediment, which projects, ſupported by Three-quarter-Columns of the ſame Order, as the Entablature and Baluſtrade of the other Parts are by Pilaſters.——
On the fourth Side this Court is a magnificent Library, 141 Feet long, built in the *Corinthian* Order, the Pillars of which are four Feet in Diameter,

PECKWATER

ter. Underneath was intended a Piazza opening
to the Square, with seven Arches, and an Ascent
of three Steps running the whole Length of the
Building. This Design has been since alter'd, for
the more convenient Reception of the great Collection of Books belonging to the College, which
is larger perhaps than that of any private Society
in *Europe*. The Arches are now wall'd up half
way, and Windows plac'd in the rest of the Space.

Canterbury Court, formerly *Canterbury* College,
is a small irregular Square, South-East of *Peckwater*, consisting of ordinary Buildings, which,
tho' they contain good Apartments, do not require
a particular Description.

The Chaplains Court is situated South-East of
the grand Quadrangle, on the North Side whereof is the old Library, which was the Hall or Refectory of St. *Frideswide*'s Priory.

The Court of the Grammar School is South of
the great Quadrangle, having the Hall on the
North Side of it, and the College Kitchen (built
by the Cardinal) on the East. On the North Side
likewise, under Part of the Hall, is the Master's
Common Room, which is very noble and spacious, in which is a superb Marble Chimney Piece,
and over it an excellent Bust by *Rysbrac* of Dr.
Busby, formerly Master of *Westminster* School,
and a great Benefactor to the College. Round
the Room are the Pictures of several of the Masters of the same School, and other eminent Men
belonging to the College. There is also an elegant
Range of Buildings, usually called *Fell*'s, looking
towards the Long Walk and the Meadows, which
contain as desirable Apartments as any in *Christ-
Church*. The Stone with which all these Buildings, and the rest of the Colleges, are built, is

K   brought

brought from *Hedington*, within two Miles of *Ox-ford*.

Next to the Buildings of *Chriſt-Church*, their long Gravel Walk, planted on each Side with Elms, deſerves our Notice, being a Quarter of a Mile in Length, and of a proportionable Breadth. This is much the fineſt Walk about *Oxford*.

'Parallel to this is another Walk under the Walls of *Corpus-Chriſti* and *Merton* Colleges, which is much reſorted to by *Invalids*, on account of its being ſhelter'd from the North Winds by the Colleges above mentioned.

This College was founded by Cardinal WOL-SEY upon the Place where formerly ſtood the Priory of St. *Frideſwide*, which, with ſeveral other religious Foundations, were diſſolv'd, in order to endow the new College intended by the Cardinal. The Deſign was far from being compleated at the Time of the Cardinal's Diſgrace, little more being built than the Eaſt, South, and Part of the Weſt Sides of the great Quadrangle, and the Kitchen. And as to the Foundation itſelf, whatever it might be at that Time, 'tis certain it was afterwards leſſen'd, and the Form of it alter'd two or three times by the King. The Diſgrace of the Cardinal happen'd in the Year 1529. when the King ſeiz'd upon this College, as well as the other Eſtates belonging to the Cardinal. In the Year 1532, at the Inſtance of Lord *Cromwell*, the King new-modell'd the Foundation, and gave it the Name of King *Henry the Eighth*'s College. This was ſuppreſs'd in 1545, and in the Year following, 1546, the Epiſcopal See was remov'd from *Oſeney* to this College, and the Church of St. *Frideſwide* conſtituted a Cathedral, by the Name of *Chriſt's-Church*.

This

This Foundation has continued in the same Form ever since. It consists of a Dean, 101 Students, *viz.* 60 to be elected by the Canons, to which Queen *Elizabeth* afterwards added 40 more, (to be annually supply'd from *Westminster School*, as Vacancies should happen in that Number) 8 Chaplains, 8 Singing-Men, and as many Choristers, a Schoolmaster, an Usher, an Organist, &c. Since the time of Queen *Elizabeth* this College has largely experienc'd the Bounty of several Benefactors, particularly Dean *Fell*, who left ten Exhibitions of 10 *l. per Ann.* to Commoners whose good Behaviour for a Year should recommend them to the Favour of the College, and to be held for ten Years from the Time they were nominated to them. Another Student was added to the 100 above by *Willian Thurston*, Esq; 1663, and is now in the Gift of the *Vernon* Family. Several Exhibitions of 13 *l. per Ann.* were given by Lady *Holford*, for Scholars educated at the *Charter-House*, and many other by different Benefactors.

This College has no other Visitor but the King or those commissioned by him; King *Henry* VIII. when he re-founded it, having appointed no special Visitor.

Late and present Dean.

1732. *John Conybeare*, D. D. Bishop of *Bristol*.
1756. *David Gregory*, D. D.

PEMBROKE COLLEGE.

PEmbroke College, so called from the Earl of *Pembroke*, Chancellor of the University at the Time it was founded, is situated near St. *Aldate's*

Church,

Church, opposite to *Chrift-Church*, and confifts of two small Courts. The Chapel is a small, but, elegant Building; and tho' feldom vifited by Strangers, this Cabinet (for fo it may defervedly be called) merits that Favour more than fome others which rarely efcape their Notice. The Mafter's Lodgings, which joins to the College on the North, is a handfome modern Edifice.

This College, formerly *Broadgate* Hall, was founded *An.* 1620, by *Tho. Tifdale*, of *Glymton*, Efq; and *Richard Whitwick*, S. T. B. for the Study of Divinity, Civil and Canon Law, Phyfic, &c.

The Charter of Incorporation expreffes it to be of the Foundatiom of King *James*, at the Charge and Expence of *Thomas Tifdale* and *Richard Whitwick*. A Charter of Mortmain alfo was granted, empowering the College to purchafe Lands of the Value of 700*l. per Ann.* Four of *Tifdale*'s Fellows to be chofen out of his Relations, and the reft to come from *Abingdon* Free-School.

As to *Whitwick*'s Benefaction, he founded three Fellowfhips and four Scholarfhips, two of the Fellows and two Scholars to be of his Name or Kindred, and the other three from *Abingdon* School.

King *Charles* I. granted to this Society the perpetual Advowfon of St. *Aldate*'s Church, and certain Lands, for the Maintenance of one Fellow, to be chofen from *Guernfey* or *Jerfey.*

Archbifhop *Abbot*, *Juliana Stafford*, and *Francis Rous*, were the next Benefactors.

Dr. *George Morley*, Bifhop of *Winchfter*, founded five Scholarfhips for the Natives of *Guernfey* and *Jerfey.*

Queen *Anne* annex'd a Prebend of *Glocefter* to the Mafterfhip: Lady *Holford* gave two Exhibitions of 20*l.* a Year each; Dr. *Hall*, Mafter of

this

this College and Bishop of *Bristol*, built the Master's Lodgings; Sir *John Bennet*, Lord *Ossulstone*, endow'd two Fellowships and Scholarships; Mr. *Townsend* gave eight Exhibitions to young Scholars from *Gloucester*, *Cheltenham*, *Northleach*, and *Camden*, *Gloucestershire*; and Sir *John Phillips*, Bart. in 1749, founded one Fellowship and one Scholarship.

The present Members are a Master, fourteen Fellows, 24 Scholars and Exhibitioners; the whole Number of Students usually about 70.

The Chancellor of *Oxford* is Visitor.

Late and present Master.

1714. *Matthew Panting*, D. D.
1738. *John Ratcliffe*, D. D.

✿✿✿✿✿✿✿✿✿✿✿✿✿✿✿✿✿✿✿✿✿✿✿✿

WORCESTER COLLEGE.

*W*Orcester College is pleasantly situated on an Eminence, just above the River *Isis*, and the Meadows at the Extremity of the Western Suburb. This is now rebuilding, and the Library actually finished, which is a magnificent Edifice, 100 Feet in Length, and built of Stone, over a Cloister, supported by Pillars. According to the Plan proposed, this College is to consist of a spacious Building. The Library on the East, the Chambers of the Fellows and Scholars on the North and South, and the Gardens, which are to lie on a Descent to the River, on the West: The Apartment of the Provost is to be at the North-

West

Weſt Angle; the Chapel and Hall to be in the Front of the College, the firſt on the Right, and the other on the Left, at the Entrance of the Gate, and to extend Weſtward to the Library; the Dimenſions of the Chapel and Hall to be the ſame, *viz.* each of them to be 50 Feet in Length, and 25 in Breadth; from whence it is eaſy to foreſee, that this College will enjoy not only the pleaſanteſt Situation, but be one of the moſt elegant Structures in this Univerſity.

This College was founded *Anno* 1714. by Sir *Thomas Cookes*, Bart. for a Provoſt, ſix Fellows, and ſix Scholars.

It was anciently call'd *Gloucefter* Hall, from the *Benedictine* Monks of *Gloucefter*, who educated their Novices here in Academical Learning. On the Suppreſſion of Religious Houſes, this was veſted in King *Henry* VIII. who granted it to Dr. *Robert King*, the firſt Biſhop of *Oxford*, for a Palace for him and his Succeſſors, and the Biſhop remained in Poſſeſſion thereof as long as the See was at *Oufeney*.

It was purchaſed afterwards by St. *John*'s College, and called St. *John Baptift*'s Hall, a Fellow of St. *John*'s being principal of it; and in 1714. was converted into a College, by a Charter obtained from Queen *Anne*.

Dr. *Finney* gave two *Staffordfhire* Fellowſhips, and two Scholarſhips. Lady *Holford* gave two Exhibitions of 20*l.* a Year each, for *Charter-Houfe* Scholars, to be enjoy'd for eight Years.

In 1739. Mrs. *Eaton*, Daughter of Dr. *Byrom Eaton*, late Principal of *Gloucefter Hall*, founded ſix Fellowſnips and ſix Scholarſhips.

Dr. *Clarke*, late Fellow of *All Souls* College, founded ſix Fellowſhips and three Scholarſhips in

1736. with a Preference to Clergymen's Sons, (*cæteris paribus*). He likewife gave 50*l.* a Year to buy Books, befides his valuable Library, which of itfelf was a large Collection, and being now depofited in this College Library renders it equal to moft.

The prefent Members are the Provoft, eight Fellows, eight Scholars, and two Exhibitioners; the whole Number between 30 and 40.

Late and prefent Provoft.

1714 *Richard Blechynden*, D. C. L.
1739 *William Gower*, D. D.

HERTFORD COLLEGE——

I S fituated oppofite to the great Gate of the Public Schools, confifting of an irregular Court, which about thirty Years ago was begun to be rebuilt. The College is intended to be erected in the Form of a Quadrangle, to confift of four *Angles*, and four intermediate Buildings; each Angle to confift of three Stair-Cafes and fifteen fingle Apartments; each Apartment to contain an outward Room, a Bed-Place, and a Study. Of thefe the South-Eaft Angle, and the Chapel in the South are already finifhed. The Principal's Lodgings are to be in the Eaft, the Hall in the North, and the Gateway (with the Library over it) in the Weft.[29]

Hertford or *Hart* Hall, an ancient Houfe of Learning, was founded by *Walter Stapledon*, Bp. of *Exeter*, *Anno* 1312. and was an Appendant to *Exe-*

ter College. But having receiv'd an Endowment
in Part, was, at the Requeſt of Dr. *Richard Newton*, then Principal, who endow'd the Fellowſhips,
incorporated, and converted into a College, *Sept.*
8, 1740. It is intended chiefly for the Education
of young Scholars deſign'd for Holy Orders, conſiſting of a Principal, four Senior Fellows or Tu-
tors, and eight Junior Fellows, or Aſſiſtants, who
have under their Care a Number of Pupils of ſeveral Denominations, *viz.* Gentlemen-Commoners,
Commoners, Students, &c. At preſent there are
about forty Members.

PRINCIPALS.

1740. *Richard Newton*, D. D. Founder.
1753. *William Sharp*, M. A.

H A L L S.[30]

THERE are ſtill five Halls remaining, which
are Academical-Houſes not incorporated;
for this it is which diſtinguiſhes a Hall from a College in *Oxford*. The Students take an Oath to obey
the Statutes and Cuſtoms of the Hall, which Statutes are made and alter'd by the Chancellor, who
has the Nomination of all the Principals, and is
Viſitor of all the Halls, except St. *Edmund* Hall;
but that remaining dependant on *Queen*'s College,
the Principal of it is appointed by that Society.

I. St. *Alban* Hall, which is in St. *John*'s Pariſh,
and adjoins to *Merton* College on the Eaſt. It was
founded by *Robert de St. Alban*, by a Grant from
King

King *Henry* VIII. out of Part of the Lands belonging to the Abbey of *Littlemore*. Of this Hall were Archbishop *Marsh*; Dr. *Lamplugh*, Archbishop of *York*; *Benedict Barnham*, Alderman of *London*, who built the Front of the Hall as it is at present; and *William Lenthall*, Esq; Speaker of the Long Parliament.

Late and present Principal.

1723. *James Bouchier*, LL. D.
1731. *Robert Leyborne*, D. D.

II. St. *Edmund* Hall is opposite to the East-Gate of *Queen*'s, to which College it is dependant, and has about 25 Students. The Buildings were completed, and other considerable Improvements made by the late Principal. Of this Hall were Dr. *John Mill*, who publish'd the *Greek* Testament, printed at the *Theatre*; and *Thomas Hearne*, M. A. that diligent Antiquarian.

Late and present Principal.

1740. *Thomas Shaw*, D. D.
1751. *George Fothergill*, D. D.

III. *New-Inn* Hall stands at the West-End of the City, and is the Property of *New College*, from whence it had its Name. It was formerly call'd *Trillock's-Inn*, from *John Trillock*, Bishop of *Hereford*, who founded it in the Year 1349. Eminent Men of this Hall were Dr. *Arthur Bulkeley*, Bishop of *Bangor*; Dr. *Rowland Merrick*, Bishop of *Bangor*; *Richard Davies*, Bishop of St. *David*'s; and Dr. *John Budden*, an eminent Civilian.

Late

Late and prefent Principal.

1732. *D'Bloffiers Tovey*, LL. D.
1744. *William Walker*, LL. D.

IV. St. *Mary* Hall ftands North of *Oriel* College, near the *High-Street*, and gives Name to the Lane leading from thence to *Chrift-Church* Back-Gate. It confifts of one fmall Quadrangle, with a Garden enclos'd in the Middle of it, which for Neatnefs may vie with any Thing in the Univerfity. It is formed by the Principal's Lodgings on the North, the Hall and Chapel on the South, and on the Eaft, Weft, and partly on the South by the Chambers of the Students.

This Hall was founded by King *Edward* II. Dr. *Dyke* gave four Scholarfhips. Some Exhibitions alfo have lately been given to affift the Students in the Profecution of their Studies.

Several very eminent Men have had their Education here, viz. Cardinal *Allen*, Sir *Thomas Moore*, *Erafmus*, Mr. *Sandys* the celebrated *Englifh* Poet and Traveller, &c.

The Number of Members of all Denominations here, (efpecially of Gentlemen Commoners) ufually exceeds that of any other Hall, amounting to about 40 in the whole; and, to do it Juftice, it has been a flourifhing Seminary for many Years.

Late and prefent Principal.

1712. *John Hudfon*, D. D.
1719. *William King*, LL. D.

V. *Magdalen* Hall is an ancient Building, adjoining to the Weft Side of *Magdalen* College, to which it is an Appendant. The Number of Exhibitions given to this Hall fupplies it with many Members.

Members. Its prefent Number of all Denominations are about 30. It was founded by *William* of
Wainfleet, the Founder of *Magdalen* College.

This Hall has had many illuſtrious Members,
viz. the Right Hon. *Edward* Earl of *Clarendon*,
Lord High Chancellor of *England*, and Chancellor
of the Univerſity of *Oxford*; Dr. *Henry Wilkinſon*,
formerly Principal; Dr. *White*, Mr. *Meeke*, Dr.
Brunſell, and Dr. *Lucy*, each of whom endow'd
this Hall with Exhibitions; Sir *Robert Hyde*, and
Sir *Matthew Hale*, Lord Chief Juſtices; *William
Tyndall*, M. A. known by the Name of *The Engliſh Apoſtle*, a Martyr for the Reform'd Religion;
Dr. *Pococke*, Dr. *Plott*, and *Edward Leigh* Eſq;

Late and preſent Principal.

1744. *William Deniſon*, ſenior B. D.
1755. *William Deniſon*, junior B. D.

F I N I S.

NOTES

1. Thomas Warton, the Younger (1728-90), was a Fellow of Trinity College, Oxford, Professor of Poetry (1757-67), and Camden Professor of History (1785-90) at Oxford, as well as Poet Laureate (1785-90). These lines are a modified version of lines from "Ode for Music, as Performed at the Theatre in Oxford on the Second of July 1751. Being the Anniversary Appointed by the Late Lord Crew, Bishop of Durham, for the commemoration of Benefactors to the University." The Ode was set to music by Dr. Philip Hayes (1738-97), Professor of Music (1777-97), for the occasion. Like *A Pocket Companion* itself, the ode was printed for R. Clements in Oxford. When he printed the *Companion*, he or Warton (they must have known each other) modified some of the lines of the ode, probably because their being quoted out of context did not make the reference to Oxford of the original version readily obvious.

2. Here and on the following page are references to the University at the time of King Alfred. Thomas Salmon is the immediate source of this myth, which has no basis in history.

3. St. Frideswide (d. 739 ?), probably the daughter of King Didanus of Oxford, consecrated her life to God and vowed lifelong virginity. She was, however, pursued by King Algar of Leicester. When he attempted to see her in Oxford, St. Frideswide sought God's help. Algar was struck blind, saving her from ravishment. Accounts differ as to whether his sight was subsequently restored. She remained in Oxford, where she founded a religious house, had a holy spring, and worked miracles. October 19 is St. Frideswide's day.

4. We will not normally footnote ruins which have subsequently disappeared, but many names, such as Beaumont and Gloucester Green, are retained in modern Oxford in the street names (Beaumont Street) or names of areas (Gloucester Green, a bus depot).

5. The beautiful river referred to is the Thames which flows on into London. There are two rivers in Oxford. One is

the Cherwell, and one is called the Isis by the locals, though it is the Thames. When the two join just south of the city, the name Thames prevails.

6. The only section of the city wall yet standing is that part mentioned above in New College. The ancient gates are remembered primarily in the names of hotels, pubs, developments, etc.

7. Most of the street names from eighteenth-century Oxford remain, but some (for example, Old Butcher-Row which is now Queen Street) have been changed.

8. Only the tower of St. Martin's (Carfax Church) is extant. Visitors may climb to the top for a good view of Oxford.

9. The street from Carfax south, passing in front of the old town hall and Christ Church, is now called St. Aldate's until it reaches Thames Street, when it becomes Abingdon Road.

10. The building now on the site of the eighteenth-century Town Hall was built in 1896 and currently houses the city museum.

11. This structure was removed during the rebuilding of the bridge in the early nineteenth century. Today the bridge is known as Folly Bridge.

12. St. Mary's remains the University Church, while All Saints has been remodelled and serves as the library of Lincoln College. St. Peter's in the East has been converted into a library for St. Edmund Hall. St. John's Church continues to be the chapel for Merton College (see below).

13. Convocation is the body that chooses some officers of the University and is made up of all holders of Master's degrees from Oxford who have maintained their status in the University. Essentially all active faculty are members of Congregation, and this body is the ultimate authority of the University. The University Exercises in the eighteenth century consisted of the granting of degrees and honorary degrees and the conducting of examinations and disputations.

14. This building is now the Museum of the History of Science. The Ashmolean Collection now shares handsome quarters in Beaumont Street with the Taylorian Institution which is devoted to the study of modern languages.

15. Most of the science departments with all of their attendant laboratories are now situated to the north of central Oxford in modern facilities.

16. The printing facilities for the University are located on Walton Street, north of Worcester College.

17. The Physic Garden is now usually called the Botanic Garden.

18. "Was blown" would be expressed in modern English as "came into bloom."

19. Please see the Appendix for a discussion of Colleges founded since 1756. St. Hilda's College, on the east bank of the Cherwell, is now the first College on the road from London, though both Magdalen and Queens Colleges have new buildings on the east side of the Cherwell.

20. During the English Civil Wars religious zealots bent upon purifying the Church from traces of Rome destroyed many ancient monuments.

21. Opened in 1748, the Old Music Room stands in Holywell Street to this day. It was the first building in England to be dedicated to musical performances alone.

22. "Demi" refers to undergraduate scholars. Their allowances were half of those of the Fellows.

23. The celebration of May Morning still occurs. The choir of Magdalen College sings from the top of the bell tower to the visitors and students assembled on the streets and in punts on the Cherwell. The revelry is enjoyed by all!

24. Each College has a visitor who is empowered to adjudicate disputes among fellows, officers, and students of the College.

25. The head of a College may be called President, Principal, Warden, Provost, Master, Rector, or Dean, in

accordance with College tradition. In each case his/her powers and responsibilities are determined by the statutes of incorporation.

26. "Without the City" means that it was outside the city walls. The Turl Gate is no longer standing, but the street name remains. Trinity College stands in the Broad, opposite Turl Street.

27. The modern visitor to these gardens would never realize that just below a part of them is a large extension, called the Norrington Room, of the Blackwell's bookshops.

28. There is a commemorative pavement in the Broad and an elaborate memorial to the martyrs between Magdalen Street and St. Giles. During the reign of Queen Mary in the middle of the sixteenth century, the martyrs were burned alive in a ditch outside Balliol College.

29. Though modern, the Bridge of Sighs (1913), which links the north and south sections of the College space, is too notable an architectural feature to be ignored. It is a replica of the bridge of the same name in Venice.

30. There are five permanent private halls not recognized as Colleges by the University. They are, however, not the same as in 1756. St. Edmund Hall is the lone independent survivor from the eigthteenth century. It became an incorporated College of the University in 1957.

APPENDIX

With the founding of Worcester College in 1714 and the incorporation of Hertford Hall in 1740, a period of stability in the development of new foundations in the University of Oxford set in. For more than one hundred years no new Colleges were endowed, probably because expansion of this sort was not required. From the founding of St. Catherine's College in 1868 until the present, however, many colleges have been established to answer, in most cases, specific needs of the University.

One obvious lack perceived by the latter half of the nineteenth century was educational opportunity for women. Another, which surfaced somewhat later, was the need to provide additional opportunity for advanced study for graduate students from Oxford and from other universities, particularly in the sciences, but in arts and letters as well. Yet another was the desirability of having several Colleges that would allow for the entry of students from less than prosperous beginnings, a need recognized during the era of social reform in nineteenth-century England. Of course, none of the newer establishments has benefitted from the rich endowments accumulated by the older Colleges over the centuries. Nonetheless, each new College has found support in many quarters, and each has increased the richness of the educational experience that Oxford University offers its students and faculty today.

The history of women in Oxford University and its Colleges has been neither long nor always happy, but today women are accorded all rights, privileges, duties, and responsibilities that other members of the University enjoy. The history of women in the University is also very confusing, and those interested should read the penetrating and sensitive account of Vera Brittain, *The Women at Oxford* (London: Harrap, 1960). Ms. Brittain makes intelligible the many controversies and difficulties of the struggle to gain the same educational opportunities for women as men had enjoyed for centuries while portraying the motivations and personalities of the women *and* men at the forefront of the movement. In 1974, five men's Colleges led the rest in accepting women at all levels, and today only two Colleges remain in the University that do not accept both men and women, at least at the graduate level, while most restrictions of a religious or social nature are no longer applied.

Students wanting to study at Oxford who have taken first degrees at other universities are now allowed to participate in the University through several new colleges that emphasize graduate education resulting in various advanced degrees or diplomas. Additionally, there are University laboratories, departments, museums, and the science library that support all areas of scientific inquiry, one of the major emphases of graduate programs at Oxford.

While a few individuals of modest means had the opportunity to study at Oxford before 1860 as scholarship students, higher education was generally a privilege available only to the well-to-do. As the various reform movements of the mid-nineteenth century gained momentum, the need for establishments that would allow for the admission and education of men from poor backgrounds was recognized. Some men of vision no longer accepted the old rule that wealth was what entitled people to attend the University. The establishing of two foundations between 1868 and 1870 (with several more to come later) answered some of the needs created when the designation of Servitor (poor student) was abolished in 1850 and diminished somewhat the University's rarified atmosphere.

The new Colleges are not situated in the center of Oxford for the obvious reason that each had to find a location after nearly all space in the city center was filled to overflowing. It will take some time and effort on the part of the visitor to see the newer Colleges, but each new College has distinct and interesting characteristics to reward the diligence of the visitor willing to wander away from the oldest parts of Oxford. Visitors who adopt an organized scheme will be able to see more of the new Colleges more easily. Such schemes, grouping together Colleges more or less near each other, are offered as the organizing principle of the descriptions and discussions that follow.

ALPHABETICAL LIST OF
NEW COLLEGES

The first itinerary includes Wolfson, Lady Margaret Hall, St. Anne's, St. Antony's, and St. Hugh's. Wolfson is probably farther from the center than any other College, but the visitor will not regret making the effort to see it. We have made no attempt to mention all the new residential buildings or institutes connected with Colleges but external from the main establishment. Both are all over the city. We anticipate that the brief introductions to the new Colleges that follow will encourage visitors to see these Colleges for themselves, especially on lovely spring, summer, or autumn days.

Wolfson College

Wolfson College, located north of the city center, can most easily be reached by bus up the Banbury Road to Linton Road. Because it is at the east end of Linton Road, the visitor will have a fine opportunity to pass through a pleasant and typical residential area in North Oxford. The final approach to Wolfson takes one into a car park, but by turning right and following the path to the bridge over the River Cherwell, one obtains a lovely view of the College. Instantly striking is how well the modern architectural style of low, white college buildings has been adapted to the exquisite site. Huge chestnut trees, sparkling flowers, and green lawns, all give the feeling of a sedate and inspiring environment for the serious scholar. Backing against the Cherwell as it does ensures the long continuation of the peaceful atmosphere while the view across the river is truly pastoral.

Founded in 1965 as Iffley College, Wolfson experienced a name change after generous donations from the Ford and Wolfson Foundations. Though there are a few undergraduates in the College, graduate education is the primary emphasis. Both women and men who have graduated from other institutions around the United Kingdom and the world gather here to pursue advanced study in many subjects, though the natural sciences seem to be of intense interest.

Leaving Wolfson, turn south on Chadlington Road and after the bend to the west turn south again, this time on Dragon School Lane. A jog to the west on Norham Road with a quick left into Fyfield Road will bring one to Norham Gardens Road and the front gate of Lady Margaret Hall.

Lady Margaret Hall

LMH, as Lady Margaret Hall is almost universally known today, has a splendid situation. The College shares a mostly southern boundary with the spacious University Parks, and the River Cherwell runs along the eastern edge of the lush and gracious gardens and lawns. Open meadows and fields provide a rural vista across the Cherwell. The secluded setting of the College reminds one that, away from the bustle and traffic of central Oxford, the opportunity for the contemplative life is still very much alive. An attempt has been made to maintain architectural unity among the buildings which are of red brick with white trim, primarily Georgian in style. The Chapel is an unusual example of Byzantine architecture, but blends in well with its surroundings.

In 1878 LMH was founded for young women members of the Church of England. It was the earliest response to the demand for equality of educational opportunity for women, and it has responded intelligently to that need ever since. LMH became an incorporated College of the University in 1926 and now affords men equal opportunity with women. The emphasis of the College is on undergraduate education, but graduate students also add their important dimension to the scholarly environment.

Leaving LHM, one comes immediately to a gate on the left that takes one to the University Parks. By taking this turning, one can stroll happily down the path on the northern edge of the Parks, admiring the many trees and shrubs along the way. The lucky visitor might happen on a cricket match on the green or a tennis game, either a pleasant recess in the pursuit of the new colleges. Continuing along the northern edge, one leaves the Parks at Banbury Road. Immediately across the Road is St. Anne's College, reached by a brief walk north to Bevington Road. The entrance is on Woodstock Road.

St. Anne's College

St. Anne's grounds are south of Bevington Road and extend from Woodstock Road through to Banbury Road. The entrance gate with its tower is quite impressive and leads one quickly into the interior of the College. The pleasant green lawn and large trees relieve the somewhat stark modernity of the newer residential buildings and the large Hall with its two glass sides and unusual dome. The absence of the traditional college quadrangle provides an air of informality and welcome lacking at some other Colleges.

Named the Society for Oxford Home Students in 1891, though loosely organized in 1879, St. Anne's was incorporated as a College of the University in 1952. The Society originally provided educational opportunity for young women who lived out of College in Oxford, but wanted to study at the University. Rather quickly these women began living in hostels and eventually formed a community of students similar to those in other halls and Colleges. Now both men and women enjoy the privilege of studying at this fairly modern establishment within an ancient University.

St. Antony's College

Just north of Bevington Road at the corner with Woodstock Road stands St. Antony's College. Though the physical configuration of the College is not extensive, it is this very compactness that gives a sense of well-being to the visitor. The lawn with its pleasant trees brings together the older chapel (now the college library) with the large, modern building housing the Hall and various common rooms. This building blends harmoniously with the modern subjects in history and the social sciences that are the emphases of St. Antony's.

The College was founded in 1948 and opened for graduate students in 1950. Students read for specialized advanced degrees or diplomas in a large number of the social sciences and enjoy the opportunity of learning from scholars who attend or take part in symposia or conferences sponsored or conducted by the College. St. Antony's provides an intimate educational experience for those whose scholarly interests are very often international in scope.

On leaving St. Antony's the visitor should again turn north and continue up Woodstock Road to St. Margaret's Road. A turn to the right will bring one to the last College on this itinerary.

St. Hugh's College

The north entrance to St. Hugh's is very unassuming because the buildings face south. The visitor is, however, quickly impressed with the red brick buildings which face gardens that abound with colorful flowers and lush trees. And, of course, because the buildings back onto St. Margaret's Road, the southern vista provides a peaceful haven that one finds surprising in a site bordering Banbury Road.

Founded in 1886 for young women, St. Hugh's was incorporated as a College of the University in 1926. It was established to provide a full range of educational opportunities for women from poor circumstances, but it soon accepted students from all backgrounds. Today St. Hugh's has women undergraduates and both men and women graduate students who pursue their studies in a secluded collegiate environment, an integral part of the University but happily remote from its center.

Buses on Banbury Road will take one back to the city center where another brief walk will take the visitor to two more new Colleges, the second of the itineraries.

For those with only a brief time in Oxford, two new Colleges very close together and surprisingly accessible from the city center are Nuffield and St. Peter's. These two Colleges will give the visitor a taste of what the more recent foundations are like.

Nuffield College

From Carfax a short walk down Queen Street brings one to New Road. The entrance to Nuffield College is near the west end of the road. Stepping into Nuffield gives one the feeling of being transported to a Cotswold village. The cream-colored buildings with gabled windows and dark roof-tiles are perfectly matched. The one unusual feature is the tower which rises several stories above the other buildings and, with its conical copper spire, is visible for miles as one of the modern additions to the "dreaming spires" of Oxford. There are two quadrangles open to the public, each with a pool where, in the right week in May, several ducks shooing their newly hatched young along add to the village atmosphere.

Nuffield was founded in 1937 for men and women graduate students wishing to pursue topics in the social sciences. Both academicians and barons of industry, trade, and politics study and read in the graduate community, each gaining perspective and insight from the ideas and experiences of the other group. It is hard to imagine a situation more conducive to serious research than this retreat from hectic modern life.

Turning back toward the city center when leaving Nuffield leads on past Bulwarks Lane to St. Peter's College.

St. Peter's College

Standing between Bulwarks Lane and New Inn Hall Street, St. Peter's, while standing on an ancient site, was founded in 1929 and incorporated as a College only in 1961. Its buildings are a diverse group, some of which were rebuilt, moved, or changed to become as they are today—for example, the chapel. The gardens are small but pleasant, and the grassy back quad provides relief from the rather crowded conditions imposed by the restraints of the site.

Originally designed to provide the opportunity of an education at Oxford for men from modest beginnings and those wishing to take orders in the Church of England, St. Peter's has no restrictions on admission today. Both men and women now study a wide variety of subjects, without the religious proviso of the past.

A third itinerary, while entailing a good bit of walking, takes in two more of the newer Colleges. From the High Street the visitor can head east past All Souls College and Queen's College to Queen's Lane. A turn to the left brings one to a new College within the old city wall.

St. Edmund Hall

Though St. Edmund Hall is mentioned in the eighteenth-century section of this guide to Oxford, it is really a new College, having had a long and difficult history. For nearly four hundred years it was owned and operated by Queen's College, but in 1937 it became an independent establishment, gaining incorporation as a College in 1957. So, while having a long tradition in Oxford, Teddy Hall, as it is called by most, is developing a distinguished modern history.

The architecture of the College today expresses well the two lives of the College. A medieval fire-place is the only remnant of the Hall's earliest history, but there are lovely sixteenth-century buildings still in use. The modern blocks are more indicative of the vigorous new life of the College. Particularly pleasant are the grounds and old graveyard within the College walls that surround what was once the Church of St. Peter's in the East (12th and 13th centuries) and houses the College library today.

Back in the High Street, the visitor should again head east, across Magdalen Bridge to Cowley Place which leads south to St. Hilda's College.

St. Hilda's College

St. Hilda's is in the enviable position of having a
beautifully scenic location along the Cherwell River.
Because the grounds embrace the river for quite some
distance, the typical quadrangle arrangement of many
Oxford Colleges is not really available for St. Hilda's.
Instead, many of the buildings are strung along the bank
and look over lawns and gardens to the river and across to
the playing fields of Magdalen College School on the
other bank. Proceeding into the College grounds for
some distance, one does find a spacious green with
buildings on three sides.

Founded as a College for women in 1896 and incorporated as a College in 1926, St. Hilda's remains one of the
two unisex Colleges in the University. The demand for
educational facilities for women kept increasing as the
twentieth century approached, and St. Hilda's was established to help answer that demand.

Six new Colleges that make a diverse and therefore
interesting itinerary will also take the visitor past some
other important University facilities. Starting from the
Broad, one should walk east down the length of pictur-
esque Holywell Street, turning north on St. Cross Road,
curving east on Manor Road and crossing an arm of the
Cherwell. St. Catherine's College is to the south at the
end of the road.

St. Catherine's College

Enjoying a lovely expanse of green lawn to the east,
with the Holywell Great Meadow rolling down to the
Cherwell, St. Catherine's architectural unity is striking.
All of the buildings are low and modern, with gardens
and walks between. The views across the meadow are
pastoral and add an air of openness to the College
facilities that others cannot duplicate.

St. Cat's, as it is commonly referred to, was established first, in 1868, to act as a matriculating society for poor students who could not afford to belong to any Hall or College. After many changes in site and organization, St. Cat's was incorporated as a College in the University in 1962. Both undergraduates and graduates study a wide variety of subjects with scientific subjects being particularly well subscribed, as one might imagine in such a modern College.

Leaving St. Cat's, the visitor should return west to the corner of Manor Road and St. Cross Road. At that corner is the modern building housing the English Faculty and Law Libraries. Continuing north on St. Cross Road, one finds Linacre College at the corner with South Parks Road.

Linacre College

Linacre's main building is a former Roman Catholic Convent. It has been complemented by a new residential building that has been built in the same style in red brick. Its grounds are not large, but the trees are lovely. Not primarily a residential College, many of its students reside in town.

Founded as an establishment for women and men wishing to pursue advanced or postgraduate degrees in any subject, it was incorporated as a College in 1965. Its members are primarily from British universities other than Oxford or foreign universities. With a new residential block, the opportunity for the exchange of ideas will expand while the further development of the collegial atmosphere will be encouraged.

Heading west on South Parks Road, the visitor is immediately in the midst of the science area. Scientific inquiry has long been an important part of the University and has been forwarded greatly by the collegial support of the science faculty members. Not wishing to continue the duplication of laboratories in each College, the University has opted to have common facilities for the science disciplines. Fellows and students of all Colleges have access to the laboratories in the various buildings which house the faculties. This is probably the closest that Oxford University comes to the typical American academic experience. Also on South Parks Road, at the southeast corner with Parks Road, is Rhodes House, the center for the Rhodes Trust, which supports the Rhodes Scholars, and the library for Commonwealth, African, and American Studies at the University. A turn north at this corner leads one to the entrance of Keble College.

Keble College

The visitor will never confuse Keble College with any other because of its distinctive architecture. While the red brick of the original buildings is not unique in Oxford, the patterns in yellow and blue brick that decorate the buildings are unusual to say the least. The grassy quadrangles around which the buildings sit are pleasant and add a second interesting contrast to the long walls of red brick, just as the ornamental work does.

Keble accepted its first students in 1870. It was associated with the Anglican Church in its early years and offered educational opportunity to men from poor circumstances. In 1952, Keble became a fully incorporated College of the University. Now membership is open to all. Primarily a College emphasizing undergraduate education, Keble nevertheless offers postgraduates the opportunity for specialized study and research.

Keble Road, on the north side of the College, leads one to Banbury Road. Crossing over the road and walking through the churchyard of the Church of St. Giles, one comes to Woodstock Road, the other major thoroughfare leading north from central Oxford. Crossing the street and walking north brings one quickly to the entrance to Somerville College.

Somerville College

A succession of quadrangles, each larger than the one before, gives a distinct character to Somerville. The third quadrangle provides a sense of spaciousness one might not expect from a College surrounded by businesses to the south and east and the huge Radcliffe Infirmary to the north. While the architectural styles differ in and among the quads, particularly the innermost with its new residential buildings to the south and west, the differences are moderated by the lovely trees, lawns, and flowers.

Somerville was founded as an undenominational establishment for women in 1879 and became an incorporated College of the University in 1926. It remains one of the two unisex Colleges today, offering, as it did when it began, educational opportunities for women of a quality at least equal to that which men were afforded. One knows that the struggles for women's education that the founders of Somerville and the other women's Colleges endured were well worth all of the battles when visiting these Colleges today.

Leaving Somerville and proceeding north past Radcliffe Infirmary, the visitor arrives at the gate of Green College.

Green College

Green College is one of the newest Oxford Colleges, founded in 1979 to support research and study, principally in clinical medicine, making it one of the most narrowly focused of the Colleges. There are some members of the College, however, who conduct their research in areas relating medicine to social and industrial studies. While the College is not large, it is quite charming with the old Radcliffe Observatory an imposing feature within its grounds. The new buildings blend quite well with the old in style and color, and the gardens provide peaceful, open spaces.

Heading south on Woodstock Road and then St. Giles, one comes to St. Cross College at the corner with Pusey Street.

St. Cross College

St. Cross College occupies the buildings formerly called Pusey House, an establishment for high Anglican theologians. The library of that earlier institution is still maintained under its original name because of its important collections, primarily theological in nature. The lovely inner quadrangle commemorates the memory of Richard Blackwell and is named for him. The stone buildings, though situated in a busy street, provide a serene and substantial setting for the College. One interesting feature of the building is its entrance door, a departure from the typical entrance gate of most Oxford colleges.

St. Cross was founded in 1965 and was named for its former location in St. Cross Church in St. Cross Road. This graduate college supports research and inquiry in many fields, and a large number of its fellows hold important university positions. Its foundation was in part a response to the need for fellowship recognition for many members of the University faculty.

On leaving St. Cross, a short walk south will return the visitor to the city center.